The Oyster K

Dedicated to oysters and oystermen, who make the real story of Apalachicola and Saint George Island possible.

Image above: A mature female oyster with a few of her two million 'spat,' very highly magnified. From Samuel Lockwood, 1874.

Front Cover: William Lee Popham in about 1910 wearing the bow tie he used for his sermons. The former evangelist established Popham's Oyster Factory No. 1 in Apalachicola in 1923.

Back Cover: Sailboats in Apalachicola Bay from William Popham's 1919 brochure promoting Saint George Island, Florida.

Non-fiction books by James L. Hargrove

With Dr. Diane Hartle and Dr. Phillip Greenspan:

> *Health Benefits of Pecans* (2013)
>
> *Muscadine Health. Healthful Benefits of Muscadine Products* (2008)

With Dr. Carolyn D. Berdanier:

> *Nutrition and Gene Expression* (1992)

The Oyster King

The Man Who Bought St. George Island

Concerning the Extraordinary Life of Apalachicola's William Lee Popham

~by~

James L. Hargrove

"All art is autobiographical. The pearl is the oyster's autobiography."

-Federico Fellini, film-maker

Image: Five stages of oyster spat on a piling.

The Oyster King

The Man Who Bought Saint George Island

A Fictionalized Account of the Extraordinary Life of Apalachicola's William Lee Popham

ISBN-13: 978-1483961040

ISBN-10: 1483961044

Published by:

Green Heron Associates
1180 West Pine Avenue
Saint George Island, FL 32328

First Edition

Acknowledgements and Notes

This book is dedicated with gratitude to visitors, residents, and especially the oystermen of Franklin County, Florida. The author particularly thanks island residents, Eunice Hartmann and Diane K. Hartle for thoughtful comments regarding the first draft.

The sermons, poems, and lectures of Reverend William Lee Popham and speeches of William Jennings Bryan were excerpted from the historical record, and are presented with only light editing. The two men met at least twice in Apalachicola, and both traveled across the United States as prominent speakers on the Chautauqua circuit. Most of the dialogue is strictly fictional, although elements were abstracted from testimony given during the trial of Popham vs. the United States.

The author is solely responsible for all errors. But then, this is a novel. Historical, yes, but a novel nonetheless.

Sea turtle drawing by Katharine Hargrove.

Table of Contents

Cast of Characters vii

Prologue ix

Act I. Florida Honeymoon 1

The Plowboy Poet 5

The Gift... 8

First Sermon Concerning Love 10

Practice Makes Perfect.. 14

Chautauqua Initiation.. 16

First Tent Meeting.. 19

Chautauqua Sunday 26

Act II. Chautauqua Talking... 35

College Daze.. 35

Stirrings in Louisville 37

Doing the Trans-Continental... 41

The Game of Chance 43

Meeting Maude 49

Intermission. Was there Sex on the Beach?........................ 54

Act III. From Preacher and Poet to 'Oyster King' 58

An Interrupted Honeymoon 58

If Once You Saw This Place, You Would Buy It!............... 61

Entering Apalachicola.. 64

First Look, Saint George Island 65

The Ancient Ones 72

Buying Saint George Island 76

Apalachicola Sermon 78

The Saint George Company 83

The Bridge that Wasn't There 87

The Oyster Growers' Cooperative Colony 93

Oystering in Apalachicola Bay 97

Act. IV. Gilding the Oyster 100

Poet, Preacher, Promoter 102

Little Sailors in the Bay 106

Romance by the Sea 112

A 'Spat' with Rivals 118

The Dignitaries 122

Things Fall Apart 128

The Trial 132

The Oystermen Speak 136

Consequences 143

Two Years in the Atlanta Federal Penitentiary 145

The Second Coming of William Lee Popham 146

Act V. *Illigitimi non carborundum*! 150

Epilogue 154

Fraud or Futurist: You Be the Jury 159

Information Sources 166

**William Lee Popham in 1910, six years
before he purchased Saint George Island.**

"Poet, Evangelist, Author, Lecturer"

Image from *Silver Gems in Seas of Gold*

Cast of Characters

Historical figures:

Virgil and Clara Popham of Big Clifty, Kentucky

William Lee and Arthur Popham, their sons

Maude Miller Estes (Popham) of Louisville, KY

William Lee Popham, Jr., born in Tallahassee

James J. Abbott, realtor from Tampa, Florida

George Saxon, Tallahassee banker

Helen Brooks Smith, Lakeland investor

Captain John Malcolmson, Canadian investor

T.R. Hodges, Florida Shell Fish Commissioner

William C. Hodges, State Senator and Popham defense attorney

Ward Greene, Atlanta newspaper reporter

Clyde Atkinson, Tallahassee attorney

Fictional characters

Reverend John Thomas, pastor of the Big Clifty First Baptist Church

Clyde Buckley, Chautauqua promoter from Louisville, Kentucky

George Summit, Naval stores operator,
Apalachicola, Florida

Carl Carver, owner of West Point Packing Co.,
Apalachicola, Florida

Typifying the enthusiasm of many visitors, three girls leap for joy on the Gulf Beaches of Saint George Island in 1952. A ferry was available by 1955, but no bridge would be built until 1965. Image courtesy of Florida Memory state archive.

Prologue

How did an "Inlander" become an "Islander"?

William Lee Popham grew up on his father's
farm and fruit orchard in Kentucky. The farm was
700 miles from the Gulf of Mexico, and the family
had never visited an ocean, much less heard of Saint
George Island. However, by age 30, William had
offered to purchase Saint George Island from a
Tallahassee banker using as equity his 19 romance
novels, books of sermons, anecdotes, and verse.

Popham's first attempt to purchase Saint George
Island in 1916 failed in the tumult of World War I,
but by 1920, he owned the island outright. He
quickly founded an empire based on land
acquisition, real estate promotion, and income
potential from oyster harvests. By 1926, he and his
wife, Maude Miller Estes, owned 60,000 acres of
land in Franklin County and claimed a net worth of
2.8 million dollars…but they became penniless in
the aftermath of a charge of federal mail fraud.

William Lee was born to Virgil and Clara
Popham on April 14, 1885 in Hardin County,
Kentucky. The nearest town was Big Clifty, about
60 miles south of Louisville. Abraham Lincoln's
birthplace and first boyhood home is just 35 miles
away next to Knob Creek. Big Clifty is a few miles
south of Fort Knox, and due north of Mammoth
Cave, the locale William chose for one of his scenic
romance novels.

The third of four surviving children (older sisters
Elizabeth and Flora Ann, and his younger brother,
Arthur), William grew up on his father Virgil's

orchard and plant nursery business. Virgil was a member of the American Association of Nurserymen and shipped his trees and fruit nationally. William was living on the farm in 1898 when the Virginia Department of Agriculture inspected and certified the orchard. Virgil had worked as a schoolteacher and merchant, but now raised apples, peaches, pears and plums. He established a post office called New Fruit, Kentucky, and shipped fresh fruit and young fruit trees across the Southeast.

Clara Popham raised her four children attentively. A striking redhead, she had a flair for conversation that her husband lacked. William remained close to his mother all his life, and seems to have inherited his oratorical gifts from her.

William was educated in a log schoolhouse, and at Sunday school in a nearby Baptist church. He loved to read and especially enjoyed home Bible study with his family. As a young boy, he had begun to write verse based on observations around the farm and youthful daydreams. He claimed that his poem, "The Babbling Brook," was published in a London newspaper when he was 11.

By the time William was a teen-ager, he had started penning moralistic stories similar to sermons he would have heard at church. It was evident even to his father that he was not preparing to become a farmer. 'Willie' wrote diligently during breaks from his work, at school, and during quiet times at home.

As William's voice matured, people commented on how sonorous and charming his speech was. His intense gaze commanded attention, and most people who knew him assumed that he was destined to join the clergy and become a preacher. As a resident of Apalachicola later noted, "Popham had a gift. When he talked, you listened."

With his future life a question mark, an observer might well have asked how a farm boy from Kentucky became, in sequence, a widely-travelled Chautauqua orator, a published poet and writer, an evangelist, an oyster enthusiast and land promoter in Florida—and finally, a convicted felon 'doing time' in the Federal Penitentiary in Atlanta. Perhaps it was fate, merely what was "in the cards," or perhaps it is evidence that God has a great sense of humor regarding the self-styled "Oyster King."

What is not clear from the deeds in Franklin County and accounts in the Apalachicola *Times* is what motivated such a young man to begin an audacious course of action-not to mention why a banker would accept a series of romance novelettes as down payment for a $30,000 loan! This "beach read" explores the motivation, steps and missteps that led to the first real estate development on Saint George Island. As much as possible, the story is told using William Lee Popham's own words, for nothing could be more revealing of his character.

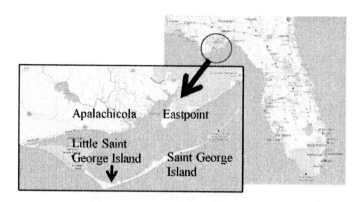

The Arc of St. George Island

For twenty-six miles, St. George Island curves along the coast of Florida offshore of the Apalachicola River delta. Seen from the sea, its gleaming white sands contrast with deep greens of pine trees and oak laurels, set off by azure Gulf water, breaking surf, and intense blue skies. Dunes of "sugar sand" rise up to 45 feet above the berm where loggerhead sea turtles crawl ashore to lay their eggs under the full moons of summer, and pelicans, ospreys and bald eagles patrol the near-shore waters.

On the bayside, marsh grasses stretch out from the island and shallow coves indent the border, creating an environment where shellfish incubate and game fish thrive. A few miles across the bay, the Apalachicola River and its tributaries spill into the bay, bringing nutrients that feed a food chain as diverse as any on earth. Salt and fresh waters exchange in tidal surges through East Pass across from Dog Island, West Pass in view of St. Vincent's Island, and Bob Sikes Cut, the shipping channel for the hamlet of Apalachicola on the bay.

In season, oyster and shrimp boats dot the bay. The oystermen arrive on the oyster bars at dawn to begin tonging with 9-foot oak handles scissored onto welded iron rakes. Except that outboard motors have replaced sails, this scene was as familiar to the Reverend William Lee Popham in 1919 as it is to modern visitors. Apalachicola Bay may be the last place in the United States where oysters are harvested by this 19th century method.

Today, the white sands of St. George Island are set off by the vivid colors of beach umbrellas and kites flying in the breezes that blow onshore during summer days. Rising above the beach are rows of colorful cottages, none more than 45 feet in height, nearly all set on ten-foot pilings that are sunk deep enough to reach solid beds of limestone. Scattered among the modern homes, a few old shacks and trailers squat on the sand on crude foundations or old poles. Most of these were ferried to the island before the bridge was built in 1965.

A tar road called State Road 300 leads from the State Park on the East end of the island along the beach through the center of a small town of perhaps 700 permanent residents to the private Plantation on the West end, and finally ends next to Sikes Cut, a shipping channel. Across the Cut, Little Saint George Island is now inhabited only by ghost crabs, seabirds, and an occasional coyote. The former lighthouse on Cape Saint George was undercut by Hurricane Opal and collapsed in 2005. The Lighthouse Association moved the bricks to the main island, and the reassembled lighthouse now presides over the hamlet of Saint George.

Except for a small hotel and the lighthouse on Cape Saint George, none of this was present when William Popham arrived in 1916. There was no bridge to the island, or, for that matter, between Apalachicola and Eastpoint. Highway 98 had not been built. People traveled to the coast by train, and reached the pristine island by sailboat or steam powered launch. They came for picnics and parties, for romantic liaisons, to fish or hunt for ducks or turtle eggs, or to enjoy relaxing by the surf. Until William and Maude Popham visited in 1916, no one had seriously attempted to develop a "City by the Sea" on Saint George Island.

Aside from the lighthouse keeper's family and guests at a ten-room hotel, the island was inhabited by wild hogs, deer, cattle, and alligators. The innkeepers mentioned the need to walk slowly along the boardwalk across the island from Nick's Hole to the beach hotel to permit sunning reptiles to move out of the way.

Starting with the founding of Apalachicola in 1831, Saint George Island had been regarded merely as a poor place to farm, raise cattle or harvest turpentine. The owners who preceded Popham were farmers and businessmen, and may not have grasped the core elements that still engender a passion for the island, its beaches, and the diverse sea life harbored in its Gulf and bay waters.

Then, in about 1919, William Popham had an epiphany. Oysters reproduce at an astonishing rate in St. George Sound. If he could just link an income from oystering with island development, people would no doubt flock to the island to enjoy the sun and surf. And so William Lee Popham became the evangelist of oystering, and wanted to convert everyone in Florida to his sentiments…as long as they could "shell out" a couple of hundred dollars down payment on land that he was able to buy using proceeds from his romance novels.

The 1852 lighthouse on Saint George Island, moved from Cape Saint George after a major storm toppled it in 2005.

Act I. Florida Honeymoon

"The first man gets the oyster. The second man gets the shell."

-Andrew Carnegie

In June, 1912, the esteemed evangelist, lecturer, poet and author Reverend William Lee Popham and his new bride, Maude Miller Estes Popham, arrived in Tampa on the Seaboard Express passenger train from Jacksonville. The Florida East Coast railway had not yet extended to the quiet fishing town of Miami on Biscayne Bay, and Tampa was best known for producing hand-rolled cigars.

The two inlanders from Kentucky honeymooned on Clearwater Beach and were taken by the sight of bathers in modest two- piece costumes who waded or swam in the gentle surf. Before long, the couple were "getting in the swim" along with the natives. Automobiles were beginning to replace horse-drawn buggies, and the honeymooners took a motor coach tour of the city and surrounding lakes and rivers.

"Will you just look at the Spanish Moss on those live oaks," Willie remarked to Maude on their tour. "This place is fabulous! What are you thinking?"

"Oh, Willie, it has been so much fun at Clearwater. The sunlight seems brighter than at home in Kentucky. The white sand beaches and pelicans diving over the breakers are delightful.   I don't want to rush back to Louisville, is there any way we can enjoy this sunshine longer?"

1

"Maude, I made enough on the last speaking tour to last a while, so there is no rush to get back. You know I have been touring for seven years, but now that we are married, it may be time to put a lid on that endeavor and find a home. I am going to ask folks back at the hotel what kind of work is available."

The couple was introduced to a personable Tampa realtor named James J. Abbott. As they discussed possibilities, he offered to show them properties in the area. "By the way, Mr. Popham, what line of work are you in?" James inquired.

"My wife and I are writers, and I have been speaking on the Chautauqua circuit since I was 17. So the billing is Evangelist, Author, Lecturer, and Poet. It may be time to look for a new line of work, though. How hard would it be to get into real estate down here?"

"No kidding, you preached on the Chautauqua circuit? Real estate is easy to get into right now; there has been a land boom ever since Henry Flagler started the Florida East Coast Railway. Frankly, I am looking for someone who could help promote my real estate interests," James replied.

Willie smiled at the mention of "promoting." "Did you ever hear of Clyde Buckley from up in Louisville? Brilliant man, he is my booking agent. He freely tutored us in the rules of the game. Clyde knows how to fill a tent, if you get my drift. I also write advertising for the circuit."

James helped Maude and Willie buy a property east of Tampa on the Alafia River. Willie named the property "Poet Eden" and immediately began planting a Satsuma orange grove so Maude could smell the blossoms every spring. He began writing advertising copy for Mr. Abbott's land promotion and publishing in Tampa area newspapers.

One afternoon in 1916, Willie mentioned to James that he and Maude had seen most of the sights around Tampa, and wondered what else they could do by way of amusement?

"You have your choice," James replied. "You can tour down Sarasota way and take in the sights. The Ringling Brothers take their circus there in the winter. Sanibel Island is a big draw if you go for seashells. That said, the most amazing place I know is in the Panhandle south of Tallahassee. The Apalachicola River runs into the bay, and just offshore there are some beautiful islands. The beaches are white sand and the surf is the most beautiful in the world, way better than Miami. For swimming and sunning, there is no comparison between the cold Atlantic Ocean and the brilliant blue Gulf."

"One of the islands is called Saint George's. It is a gem; it fronts on the Gulf of Mexico. No development on it but one little hotel and a lighthouse. People fish and hunt, and the oysters in Apalachicola Bay are the best in Florida."

James looked at his partner and added, "If you ever saw Saint George Island, you would want to buy it!"

"Say no more, James. If you don't mind, Maude and I will swing up that direction when business slows down and have a look for ourselves."

The citizens of Apalachicola had endured tropical storms, yellow fever, a Civil War blockade, a fire that burned the entire waterfront, and the hurricane of 1915. Despite all that tumult, the seafood workers and lumbermen of Apalachicola were not prepared to meet a dreamer on the scale of the charismatic William Lee Popham. More than any other person in its history, he was to change the future of Apalachicola.

Saint George Island beach scene in modern times. Dogs enjoy the surf as well as their masters—maybe more so!

The Plowboy Poet

William Popham's journey to Saint George Island began unknowingly, as a boyhood dream on the Popham farm and orchards south of Louisville, Kentucky. One May in 1900, Virgil Popham put a hand on his teen-aged son's shoulder and said, "Willie, we'll need to start planting our corn this week. Tomorrow after school, won't you hitch up one of the horses and get started plowing the bottomland down by the branch."

"I will, Papa," Willie replied. "Would you mind if I did some writing when the horse needs a rest? I love that creek, a poem always comes to mind when I am near it."

Virgil sighed, knowing better than to argue about writing with his oldest son. "Not at all, if you get the plowing done and are caught up on your school work. You will need to be good at reading, writing and figuring numbers if you want to be a partner in our family orchard business."

The next day, Willie began a ritual that would continue all year. He packed a bag with a sharpened pencil, a tablet of lined ledger paper, and a sandwich. He went to the hand pump to fill a jug of water, and headed to the barn. He put the plowing tack on the family's draft horse and led it along the creek to the fallow field his father wanted to work. After an hour of plowing, he took a break and let the horse graze along the creek.

Taking a drink of water, Willie got out his notepad and pencil. As he had plowed the field, Willie had been watching clouds drift over the line of trees in the creek bottom, and thought they must resemble surf breaking on a beach. He had already started composing a poem, and began to write quickly.

By the Surging Sea

I like to stand on golden sand

And see the waves retreat;

For on their tide the vessels ride

And the rolling waves are fleet.

Like unique things with mammoth wings

The ships are coming in;

And here I sit and thoughts commit

Of where the ships have been.

Before our doors from distant shores

O'er a trackless road

Comes the freight in value great

And at our docks unload.

The ships go back o'er watery track,

Leaving the waves for me;

And let my pen proclaim to men

My thoughts by the surging sea.

William tucked the notepad back into his shoulder bag and returned to the field. Just before sunset, he unhitched the horse, watered it at the creek, and led it back to the barn. He headed back to the farmhouse only after currying the horse and giving it extra feed.

Clara was getting supper ready, and asked Willie to help his sisters set the table. They called the family to supper, bowed their heads, and said grace before beginning their evening meal.

"So, Willie, how much plowing did you accomplish? And did you have time for any writing?" asked his mother.

"Oh yes, I ploughed an acre or so, and did write a poem. It is about the seaside."

"The seaside?" asked his father. "That is interesting, as it must be five hundred miles to any ocean. Your Mother and I have never been to the beach."

"After supper, could you read us your poem?" Clara asked. In the days before electricity, evening activities usually consisted of Bible study by the light of an oil lamp, conversation, and light work.

Willie gladly read his poem. When he finished, his mother commented, "Your voice is truly becoming a man's. It is enchanting to hear you express yourself so well."

"If you keep day-dreaming like that, you may well be travelling," said Virgil. "But keep in mind, I can always use your help with the orchard. When you are 17, I will start paying a man's wage, 75 cents a day, if our income permits it."

The Gift

Willie's parents observed that every evening, he tended to finish his school work as quickly as possible to spare time for writing. His father paid an allowance that Willie spent on writing supplies, diaries, and ledgers that he kept in a chest in the room he shared with his brother, Arthur. The farm was a mile from town, and recreation outside of school was devoted to fishing or games played with Arthur and their sisters, Elizabeth and Flora Ann.

In April, 1900, just before Willie's 15th birthday, Reverend John Thomas told the Sunday school class that they should choose one pupil to prepare a lay sermon that would be presented two weeks hence. The class unanimously selected Willie. He was the oldest student and his knowledge of scripture was remarkable, rivaling even the minister's children.

When Clara learned of the event, she advised her son, "I know that we expect the Lord to provide words of testimony. But when Reverend Thomas prepares a sermon, he always selects a Bible verse, prays for guidance, and then writes out his thoughts. You love to write, why don't you prepare as he does?"

Willie was thrilled at the idea. "What subject do you think I should choose, Mama?"

"That which is closest to your heart. What do you think?"

"I think of the love you and Papa show our family, and the hard work you do each day," Willie replied honestly. "And at church, I think of how much God loved us that he would send his Son to be sacrificed to pay for our sin."

"With that in mind, your choice should not be difficult, given all the examples of God's love in the New Testament. I am sure the congregation will find your words moving."

First Sermon Concerning Love

When the next Sunday arrived, Reverend Thomas led the congregation in prayer and hymns until the time he normally presented his sermon.

"Today we have a special treat. The Sunday school class has selected young Willie Popham to speak concerning his own testimony and thoughts about the Good Book. Lay ministry is part of our faith, and I truly look forward to hearing this. Willie, will you come forward? The pulpit is yours for the hour!"

Members of the congregation chuckled as Willie, dressed in his best Sunday suit and a red bow tie, earnestly made his way out of the family pew and walked up the steps to the pulpit. He removed a folded sheet of paper from his vest pocket and smoothed it on the lectern.

"Reverend Thomas, Brothers and Sisters, thank you for asking me to speak today. I have chosen the topic of love, and my Bible verse is John 4:8. "He that loveth not knoweth not God, for God is love." And when I think of love, it is you, the members of this congregation, to whom my thoughts go first."

"I am frank to say that I do not understand my subject, for it is the mystery of mysteries. But God does not require us to fully understand now, for the Book says, "Now we see through a glass darkly; now we see in part. . . . But in heaven we shall see face to face and know even as we are known."

Willie saw that the men had stopped smiling and were listening attentively. He raised his voice a bit so families in the farthest pews could hear.

"So we must not flatter ourselves now to think that we are very wise. I am ignorant now, and not until I enter the golden gate of heaven do I expect to fully understand what Love is."

"Do you believe in God as the Author of Love? Of course—for He first loved us sinners and sent our Savior. The fruits of Love are beauty, grandeur, harmony, sacrifice, nobility, service, humility and peace. Have you any of these signs of Love? The Good Book says if you have not Love, you have not God."

Pausing for a breath, Willie contemplated the changes taking place across Kentucky as the 19th century gave way to the 20th. He continued,

"Love is the gentlest thing in the world, and yet the most powerful. The electric current that flashes messages across the continent or from one country to another under the ocean is a silent but swift messenger, only surpassed by the wonderful system of wireless telegraphy, whose steeds are waves of mystery. Yet the silent but powerful thought currents, passing from mind to mind, the actuality of Love born in the heart and mind of man, are still more powerful than all of these."

"Thoughts are the building material of life. If the home of your soul is filled with beautiful thoughts, care, pain and poverty cannot disturb you. Then believe in love, trust love, think love, and thus love will possess your life and you will then begin to enjoy its activity. Love is the river of life in this world."

Willie continued to speak earnestly and honestly, by now aware that no one was coughing and no adult turned away from his gaze.

"When two souls come together, each seeking to magnify the other, each, in a subordinate sense, worshiping the other; each helping the other; the two flying together so that each wing-beat of the one helps each wing-beat of the other — when two souls come together thus, they are lovers."

"Love, like the tide, is confined to no shore. Love rises above waves of difficulty, sweeps through unsafe channels, braves storms and faces death, and is never satisfied till love meets love. Love can be driven out of the human heart; but like a, sunbeam, it cannot be imprisoned; it is the echo of its own voice, which brings love from another who has been enchanted by its melody."

"Friends, may Love fill your hearts, possess your minds and guide your lives over the troubled waters of life's great sea; thus the wings of love will carry you over the dark valley of death to the beautiful mansions of God where the only law is love. Jesus died because God so loved, and the only way to heaven is to love Him in return. There is no other way. Remember that Jesus is our receipt of God's grace, and if we trust and believe in Him, the heavenly door of love stands ajar to receive us."

As Willie ended his sermon, he looked up from his notes and saw that some listeners were dabbing their eyes with kerchiefs. "And this concludes my thoughts on love and the Book of John. Thank you for listening, Brothers and Sisters. Amen."

Clara looked up at Virgil, her eyes framing a question. Virgil shook his head, never having heard his son speak in this way. "I am going to have a hard time turning that boy into a farmer," he whispered.

It is not customary to clap in church, yet a gentleman near the back rose in his seat and said, "Well spoken, young man!", and began to clap. Several others stood and some joined in the applause. Reverend Thomas quickly joined Willie by the pulpit, put one hand on his shoulder, and asked the congregation to join him in a prayer of thanks.

After a brief prayer, he signaled the organist to begin a recessional, and called for the congregation to rise as he led the way to the foyer. He and Willie stood together to shake hands with people as they left the church.

As the Popham family filed past, the Reverend commented, "I don't need to tell you that Willie's sermon was as fine as any I have ever heard. Perhaps we could discuss whether it is possible for him to study at a seminary. I hope you won't mind if I make inquiries among my associates and then come visit at your farm."

Practice Makes Perfect

Reverend Thomas stopped by the Popham farm the next Saturday afternoon, and Virgil invited him in. The family was at home finishing a lunch break after a morning in the orchards.

"Virgil, I was very impressed by Willie's sermon last Sunday, and have been doing some thinking, as I am sure you have as well. Writing and speaking seem to be your son's gifts, and there are ways he could hone those skills."

"What are your thoughts, Reverend? You must know how much we depend on the boys to help work in our orchard and care for our livestock."

"Well, yes, I have some idea of how much work your business requires. On the other hand, after the crops and fruit have been tended, work is not as intense until harvest. Is that true?"

"To some extent. There are always chores to be done. We have a small flock of sheep that must be watched, there is hoeing in our cornfield and garden patch, wood to chop, produce to put up, and my mail order business for seedlings keeps us busy."

The Reverend nodded, "Yes, and you do all this labor while I minister to the congregation or work in my study. It hardly seems fair. But I was thinking of the Chautauqua Association that tours Kentucky in the summer. Speakers who are up to the task can earn a good income if they do not mind traveling."

Virgil looked away, unconvinced. "We attended a revival meeting last July. I had not imagined

Willie doing that. Clara and I could discuss the idea."

Reverend Thomas turned to Willie, "Young man, can you imagine yourself speaking to an audience in that way? You would earn part of the proceeds. I imagine you will graduate from our school next year, and I would also encourage you to think about college. Lynn College is just a day's ride over in Buffalo, and then there is the Baptist Seminary in Louisville. It is a short trip by train."

Willie sat up in his chair and replied earnestly, "Do you really think so, Reverend Thomas? Papa says my writing sometimes gets in the way of our work, but I do need to think about what I will do when I leave home. Much as I hate to think about that." He turned to his mother and felt a rush of emotion.

"I have some contacts in the Kentucky Chautauqua Circuit," the Reverend replied. If you all do not mind, let me make inquiries. I can at least get information and make introductions, and you can decide for yourselves what is best. I certainly do not mean to meddle, and only want you to know there may be possibilities."

After Reverend Thomas left, Virgil asked his son to come outside with him. He pointed to the orchard and fields, the nursery building and the packing shed.

"Willie, you know our family business. You are turning 16 this year, ready to take on a man's work. It is true that I can run the place for another ten years or so, but I could really use your help. "New

Fruit" could become "Popham and Sons," and when I get too old to work, you and Arthur could take over. There is enough business here to support two families."

Willie spoke tearfully, "Papa, you know how much I love our farm. This has been the best place to grow up I can imagine. You and Mama have given me the best upbringing a boy could have. I mean it."

"This summer is a cross-road for me, and I pray about what to do every night. The Lord has not given me any signs, beyond my love for our family, the orchard, and for my writing. Please don't be discouraged, but I must find my own way, and I can't tell you today what that will be."

Chautauqua Initiation

At the end of May, 1901, a horse-drawn buggy carrying Reverend Thomas with a stranger at the reins came along the road from town. Virgil stepped down from the porch to greet the men.

"Virgil, I would like you to meet Mr. Clyde Buckley of the Louisville Chautauqua Assembly. "Clyde, this is Virgil Popham, a prominent member of our church. He is the father of the young orator I mentioned." Virgil invited the visitors onto the porch while Clara went to the kitchen to fill water glasses.

"The Reverend has told me how impressed he is with your son's abilities, not only to speak but to compose poetry and stories. He has also told me about how hard your son works around your nursery."

Virgil nodded, "Clara and I are proud of Willie. He has an aptitude for speaking, no question about it."

"I hope you won't mind if I get right to business," Clyde said as he took a glass of water from Clara. "Doubtless you know about the Louisville Chautauqua Assembly. We have a program scheduled for the week of June 28th in Elizabethtown. Trost's band will provide music, and in the evening, President Patterson of State College will deliver a lecture complete with images projected from a magic lantern! "

"We are always seeking inspirational lecturers for our program. The idea is to promote Kentucky's progress along with good morals by telling stories and humorous or uplifting anecdotes. There will be some preaching, but the thing I am looking for is a young man with a strong voice who can tell compelling stories. Do you think your son might fill the bill?"

"Well, let's ask him about it." Virgil sent Flora Ann to call William in from the orchard. "Tell Arthur to come in too."

As Clyde shook hands with William, he noted the young man's strong handshake and his intense, focused gaze. "I must say, you have the looks of a young man who could hold an audience's attention."

William looked towards his mother as he replied, "Speaking at school or in church has never bothered

17

me as long as I warm to the subject. I have been writing poems for years, and also have been collecting anecdotes concerning famous people."

Clyde responded, "My association operates a permanent Chautauqua Assembly in Louisville and a speaking circuit around Kentucky, down to Florida and up to Washington, D.C. What I suggest, if you are interested, is to ride up Friday afternoon, and give a talk Saturday. If it works out, you might also speak on Sunday. We will put you up at the hotel and provide board, plus a share of the gate for your expenses."

William thought about his chest full of ledger paper with stories he had collected all through school, and nodded his head. "If it is okay with Father and Mother, I am willing to try."

"Well, all right," Virgil conceded. "You and Arthur can take the buggy to town for that weekend. I will give you a list of supplies you can pick up from the hardware store so the trip isn't wasted."

Buying tickets for a Chautauqua Lecture as the 20ᵗʰ century began. Before radio and television, many people attended lectures for entertainment and to improve their knowledge.

First Tent Meeting

Elizabethtown, Kentucky, is the Hardin County Seat and a railroad junction for a line that runs to Louisville forty miles north and southeast to Knoxville. William and Arthur crossed the tracks at the railroad depot and turned on Main Street. Both boys had delivered fruit trees to the depot for shipping, and knew the route.

Arthur left William at the hotel with their luggage and headed to the livery to leave their horse and buggy. Along the street, he saw colorful broadsides advertising the Chautauqua event. On his walk back to the hotel, he saw that the Saturday program listed "William Lee Popham, Kentucky's Boy Poet." He checked directions to the meeting tent, and observed that the town was busier than usual.

Clyde had indeed made arrangements for room and board at the hotel, and left two tickets with instructions to come down to the tent after they were settled. After a quick meal at the hotel, the boys walked over and got in line at the entrance. People were paying twenty five cents for the evening, or buying a $1 ticket for the weekend program.

To the boys' eyes, the tent was enormous. "This place is bigger than our church, Willie. I bet it can fit 500 people. Do you think you're ready to do this?" Willie took a deep breath. "Brother, I have to be. I promised Reverend Thomas and Mr. Buckley. Oh, look at all the people coming in!"

They found Clyde and shook hands. "Boys, I am delighted you made it, take a seat near the front and enjoy the show!"

Clyde introduced President Patterson at dusk, as the interior of the tent was getting dim. A light began to glow at the back of the tent and the magic lantern began to project an image onto a screen behind the speaker. A large machine with what appeared to be a flywheel and wires running to a glowing bulb appeared on the screen.

"This, ladies and gentlemen, is an electric generator. Some of you may have read about this, and we have men at State College working to provide our campus with electric lights! Across Kentucky, most of us rely on oil lamps and light from the hearth to do our work before bed time, but I assure you, within your lives, you will light your homes with Thomas Edison's incandescent bulbs!"

After the speech, the audience stood up, whistled, clapped and cheered. The boys stared around, wide-eyed. "Oh, Willie, I will pray for you tonight. I can't imagine standing in front of all those people and being able to speak!"

Willie's first talk was Saturday afternoon. Clyde had asked for a short anecdote that would warm the crowd before a featured speaker took the podium. Willie dressed in his Sunday best, put on his red-and-white striped bow tie, and tucked his notes into a jacket pocket. At the appointed time, Clyde asked Willie if he was ready, and asked him to come to the stage.

"Ladies and gentlemen, won't you join me in welcoming a gifted young orator who was raised on a farm right outside of Elizabethtown! Willie Popham is well known at his church down in Big Clifty. He tells me he has an edifying story concerning temperance, let's say hello to young William!" There was light applause as Willie stepped to the middle of the stage. The tent was half full, and Willie could make out families sitting together in the stands.

Willie smiled broadly and looked across the audience. The people looked back at him, curious that a boy stood before them. They looked much like families he knew from church. His pulse settled down and he took a deep breath. "Brothers and Sisters, I promise to keep my remarks brief, and when I am done, the band will play a rousing tune. I assure you, no matter how eager you may be for the band to start up, I am twice as eager!" He could hear a few chuckles in the audience.

"My first topic is one I call, Lincoln's Promise. You may know he was born within 35 miles of Elizabethtown, right over at Knob Creek. It is fitting that we recall one of the lessons he took to heart."

"While a member of Congress, Abraham Lincoln was once criticized by a friend for his seeming rudeness in declining to test the rare wines provided by their host. The friend said to him: "There is certainly no danger of a man of your years and habits of becoming addicted to the use of wine.""

Willie deepened his voice, seeking to imitate an older, wiser man.

"I mean no disrespect, John," answered Lincoln, "but I promised my precious mother only a few days before she died that I would never use anything intoxicating as a beverage, and I consider that promise as binding to-day as it was the day I gave it."

"But," the friend continued, there is a great difference between a child surrounded by a rough class of drinkers and a man in a home of refinement."

"A promise is a promise forever," answered Lincoln, "and when made to a mother it is doubly binding."

"And so I respectfully say to all of you, be careful of what you say to your Mothers, as you will need to live by your words the rest of your lives!"

Some of the audience smiled and nodded at his words, others clapped. A few more people had joined the audience and the applause was distinctly louder than during Clyde's introduction. Willie glanced at Clyde and saw that he was nodding in approval.

"Don't you think that is a good story?" Willie asked. "I certainly do. During my school days, I have written poems and stories whenever there was a quiet moment, such as when I would rest the horse whenever we plowed the cornfield. And yes, I really was bare-footed! Here is another thought that came to me in a moment of reflection."

"Every man is a king in some particular, be it ever so small. There is a good spot in the very worst of criminals. When you discover a weakness in your friend don't exaggerate it by discussion of what a pure-souled fellow Jones or Brown is; man doesn't like to be forever preached to, because he intuitively knows that his friend-preacher has faults of his own. Praise his good traits and he will become so ashamed of the bad ones that he will shed them like water from a duck's back."

Willie's voice was warm and melodious. He modulated it, sometimes speaking softly to barely carry to the back rows, other times increasing tempo and intensity so that even people in line outside could hear him.

"Isn't it true that comparisons make more enemies than friends? Water a flower and it grows; cultivate a man's good traits and they flourish. Every man has good in him which can be made to regenerate his whole being. Some thieves would shrink from murder; some liars would cower from the thought of stealing; some tattlers of tales would scorn the thought that they are liars; so it is with all mankind, for each of us has some little fault which hangs its head in misery when brought to notice the greater faults."

"Of course, I realize that none of you has a fault, as you are all law-abiding, church-going Christians." Heads nodded, and there were a few chuckles in the audience. "And even if that is not the case, you know that belief in Our Savior redeems you of your sins."

"Now I know that you are REALLY eager for the band to strike up a tune! Mr. Buckley introduced me as a poet, so let me close with a poem I wrote during a moment of reverie in the fruit orchards on my father's farm. I call it, Knowing Comfort."

> There is never a cry in all the world
> But Jesus hears the weeping;
> There is never a child of woman's birth
> But the care of God is keeping;
> There is never a word in secret prayer
> But brings our blessings nearer;
> There is never a sorrow of human life
> But makes high heaven dearer.
> There is never a song of the nightingale
> But the joys of life it's voicing;
> There is never a spoken word of love
> But sets the heart rejoicing;
> There is never a cloud across the sky
> But somewhere the sun is shining;
> And let us believe that the clouds of life
> Will leave a silver lining.

"I hope you have enjoyed my presentation as much as I enjoyed being here with you. Now, let's bring Mr. Buckley back to introduce Trost's Band!

As Willie bowed and Clyde stepped back onto the stage, many men in the audience stood and clapped. Just as at church, some of the women had taken out handkerchiefs and were dabbing tears from their eyes.

"Well done, lad, well done! Tell me after the show if you could talk a bit longer tomorrow, even up to an hour! And you must ask your father if you could join us in Louisville next season!"

Willie nodded and said, "Tomorrow, I can talk about what it was like to grow up on Father's farm." Clyde shook his hand, and asked the audience to stand and stretch their legs while Trost's band segued into "The Anvil Chorus".

Chautauqua Sunday

Neither Willie nor Arthur slept well that night. Willie pulled a stack of ledger paper from his suitcase and located his draft of a talk called "Youthful Dreams on a Farm." He read it carefully and marked a few changes to the text to make it easier to speak to an audience.

"All this time, I thought you were only day-dreaming," Arthur said. "I could never see any purpose to all your writing."

"Any more than I could," answered Willie. "Writing is just what I like to do, same as some boys like to whittle. It settles my mind."

"Well, I wouldn't worry too much about tomorrow," replied Arthur. "The audience liked you every bit as much as President Patterson. And he had a picture show!"

The boys climbed into bed and slept fitfully. The next morning, they joined Clyde and went to church together. The Chautauqua would conclude Sunday afternoon.

Willie freshened up after church but did not change out of his Sunday suit. He put on the same red-and-white bow tie that he had worn the night before, tucked his notes into his vest pocket, and headed for the tent.

A printed handbill outside the tent listed the afternoon's presentations. Next to it was a handwritten placard, reading "4 O'clock Special. Our own Plow-Boy Poet, William Lee Popham. "Youthful Dreams on a Kentucky Farm."

Willie was next to the last speaker. When Clyde called him to the stage, the tent was at full capacity. Willie's hands shook for a moment before he gained control of his breathing. After Clyde's introduction, he greeted the audience and began:

"Go where you will, the world over—but you will never find a sweeter sentiment of human life than youthful dreams on a farm. The mocking din of the city, the roaring billows of the ocean, the evening party of a quiet village where the young people assemble to relate their youthful joys, the summer gathering on the surging shores of the sea—all these fade into vapor in comparison with a country boy's blissful dreams."

"Dreams of love, dreams of hope, dreams of manhood and dreams of greatness—all these belong to the sunburned, freckled, sore-toed farm boy—as you and I know from our own experience!"

Some of the audience smiled at Willie's reference to a sore-toed boy, as few of them had worn shoes before the age of ten. Willie smiled back and returned to his favorite theme of love.

"Ah, dreams of love! Is young love a dream, or is it earnest?—those moonlit walks upon the hills by the side of a rosy-cheeked maiden, when you watch the stars, listening to her voice, and feel the pressure of that girlish hand upon your arm?"

"When you drain your memory of its whole stock of poetic beauties to lavish upon your sweetheart's ear, is it love, or is it boyish fancy?—when you catch her eye as it beams more eloquence than all your moonlit poetry, and feel an exultant gush of the heart that makes you proud as a man—even now to think of it—and yet then, a modest, timid boy beside her. Oh! the bliss, to walk beside a blushing maiden on the green lawns that lie among the swelling hills."

"One night when you "got left" you came home from the party alone. The other fellow has "asked first." Ah! Your heart almost melted all the way home. The whole world seemed dark, yet the stars and moon were shining brightly. And yet—it is very strange—she does not reproach you; there is a sweet, soft smile upon her lip,—a smile, that will come to you in your fancied troubles of later-life with a deep voice of reproach."

"Altogether you grow into a liking of the country; your boyish spirit loves its fresh, bracing air, and the sparkles of dew that at sunrise cover the hills; and the wild river, with its black-topped, loitering pools. You love the hills, climbing green and grand to the skies, or stretching away in distance their soft, blue, smoky caps. You love those oaks, tossing up their broad arms into the clear heaven with a spirit and strength that kindle your dawning pride and purposes for a kindred spirit and a kindred strength."

"The boy grows into manliness, instead of growing to be like men. He claims—with yearnings of brotherhood—his kinship with Nature; and he feels in the mountains his heir-ship to the Father of Nature."

"Ah! Here come the beautiful dreams of life! The farm house is the cradle of your dreams; and when you wake in dreamland, tell the dreams of your desire to the world and men will make your dreams come true. No man was ever born great— not even the Son of God. But boyhood dreams—I mean hope dreams, have inspired many a youth to greatness, fame and a useful life. I *like* dreamers, for I *am* a dreamer!"

"Call it dreams, aspirations, hopes or mere fancies—but let every youth be a dreamer. Dreams are ideals unrealized. If the mind is pure, dreams are signs, not of unholy ambition, but of splendid aspirations. I haven't much faith in the boy's future who has no grand dreams of what his life is to be. They are tokens of hidden power. A dreamer has within himself the conquering spirit to do and dare."

Willie began to build to a crescendo, repeating phrases for emphasis just as he had heard Reverend Thomas do at church.

"Dream on, ye stalwart youths! Yet, some of thy dreams shall be fulfilled. But not until your young soul has been seasoned in the fiery furnace of toilsome, ragged, loyal manhood. In the dense darkness of temptation, let your character show the brightest. Prove your splendid qualities by your every deed."

"Dream on!-dear youth, for the glowing hopes, born in childhood, shall call you upward and hover around you like protecting angels. A dreamer is made of heroic stuff. The sun of prosperity shall dawn upon the morning of his career. Usefulness shall crown his efforts. Joy shall fill his heart. Happiness shall sweeten his life. Obstacles shall fade away like the fog before the sun."

"Dream on!--Noble youth—for thy dreams of hope, like the evening stars, shall reflect light from heavenly skies. Dream with me, young men, dream on!" Willie declaimed and gestured towards the audience, bowing as he concluded his speech.

For a moment, the audience was quiet, but then began clapping steadily. Willie heard someone yell, "Atta boy!" while others whistled and hooted.

Clyde leapt to the stage, vigorously shook Willie's hand, and turned to the audience, "Well now, what do you think about our own Bluegrass Poet? How about one more hand!"

The audience rose and cheered. Willie bowed and repeated, "Thank you, my privilege, thank you." Arthur sat in the front row, shaking his head and looking stunned at the response. Before introducing the next speaker, Clyde called for an intermission and signaled the band to play. He told the boys that they were welcome to stay for the rest of the program, or go back to the hotel to prepare for the trip home in the morning.

Later that evening, as the boys packed their belongings, Clyde Buckley knocked on the door.

"William, you presented a fine talk on Saturday and expanded that to an hour on short notice for today. I want you to know that if you should choose to do it, there will be a place for you in next summer's circuit. We will be traveling from Kentucky to the nation's capital, on down to the Hall of Brotherhood in Florida and back up through Georgia. Please think about it, talk it over with your folks and let me know. Here is my business card that shows how to get in touch."

"You did work for me and I do my best to share the gate receipts with our speakers. You show promise, so I am actually going to up the ante a bit. Please accept these bills as payment for your work, and here is something for Arthur too. It was excellent to have your brother supporting you! Remember, I will cover the room and board that you shared. You can head home as soon after breakfast as you wish."

Arthur's eyes opened wide at the sight of two five dollar bills and a pair of two dollar bills. Fourteen dollars was a month's wage on their farm. Willie took the bills and shook Mr. Buckley's hand.

"You have given me a lot to think about," he replied, "Including whether I should attend college or go to work in Father's business. I will talk to Papa and let you know. "

I really look forward to hearing from you," Clyde replied. "I mean that. As you leave, there will be a let-down; right now you are probably feeling high as a kite. My offer is a promise, given in the same sense you mentioned in your Saturday talk. Have a safe ride home and send me a letter when you settle on your plans."

It was a two-hour ride home and the boys were tired from jolting along in the buggy by the time they reached the farm. Clara saw them coming up the lane and called to Virgil. "Well, well, the travelers are home! Boys, put the horse in the barn and you can tell us all about your trip."

31

Currency paid to William Lee Popham by promoter Clyde Buckley for his first Chautauqua lecture in 1901. The five dollar bill represents "Electricity" presenting light to the world with President Grant and General Sheridan on the reverse. The $2 bill depicts "Science" presenting Steam and Electricity to Commerce and Manufacture. As William and Arthur rode home in their horse-drawn buggy, both understood how rapidly their world was changing.

Arthur could not contain his excitement. "Willie really warmed up the crowd, Papa. I wish you could have seen them clapping and cheering, I almost fell out of my seat."

Back inside the house, Willie tried to keep his demeanor. "That Mister Buckley was as good as his word, Papa. He paid us for our work. Let me show you what he gave us. Come on, Arthur."

The boys put the $14 on the kitchen table and saw both parents react. "What, he gave you that for making a speech? That's a month's wage! I don't understand."

"Well, we got in line and saw that people were paying 25 cents for a show or a dollar for the whole set. It was a big tent, probably five hundred people, and it was sold out on Sunday."

"There's more to tell, but maybe we better be sitting down. Mr. Buckley says he could use me for next summer on the whole circuit, if you and Mama are willing."

Virgil leaned back in his chair, folded his hands behind his head, and sighed. "Willie, I want you to work with me on the farm. You know our operation, and there is no one who could replace you just like that."

"That said, you are reaching your manhood and you need to be making your own decisions about your future. Just give me some time to think about it. Remember, until now, you had been talking about attending the seminary."

"On the way home, we talked about a lot of plans," Arthur spoke. "Willie said he might want to go to college but wondered if he should try Chautauqua too. And I told him that kind of thing was not for me, but I am interested in studying Law. I am also thinking about Louisville."

Virgil assimilated the conversation more quietly than the boys had expected. Both had been worrying how to explain their thoughts to their parents. "We all have a lot to pray on," he finally said. "You know I taught school and sold hardware before we bought the farm. You never know, there might be something for me in Louisville too."

Act II. Chautauqua Talking

"I do not weep at the world. I am too busy sharpening my oyster knife."

-Zora Neale Hurston

College Daze

In 1902, Virgil surprised the family by selling his farm and moving them 60 miles north to Louisville. He used proceeds from the sale to start a manufacturing business with two partners.

Willie first got a job as a bicycle messenger for a local company and then started making special deliveries for the U.S. postal service. He enrolled in Southern Baptist Theological Seminary but attended classes only when he was off work. When Arthur finished high school, he enrolled in pre-law at Louisville University.

At the end of Willie's second semester at the Southern Baptist Seminary, his Theology professor told him that the Dean wished to speak with him. He made an appointment for the next day after work and reported to the Dean's office promptly.

Fifteen minutes after the appointment was scheduled, the Dean's secretary invited Willie into the main office. "Come in, young man, and take a seat. You might imagine I have questions for you, I need to understand your goals."

"I have spoken with several of your professors. They tell me that you are seldom in class and have not taken your exams."

Willie shrank in the chair opposite the Dean's massive oak desk. "Yes sir, I will be happy to explain. First off, I have to work to pay my tuition, and I have a day job with the post office. I come to class whenever I am free from work."

"When you applied, we had heard that you were an avid reader, a disciplined writer, and a distinguished speaker for such a young man. Your references were top notch. The admissions committee was unanimous in selecting you. This is not so much a question about your abilities; it is about lack of progress. May I ask if you have a clear goal and if perhaps you feel called to the ministry?"

"When I applied, I felt drawn to the ministry. I am not sure I have felt a calling, but I had spoken to my minister in Big Clifty many times."

"Has something changed in your life, other than the need for tuition? The Seminary might be able to help if that is the only problem."

"Well, yes sir, something has changed. Mr. Clyde Buckley has let me join his Chautauqua circuit. When I speak at the hall, there is such a response, it is hard to describe. I know that ministering to people requires a kind of selflessness. And I do question if that is my strong suit. What thrills me is the ability to promote my ideas. I do care about other people but right now, I can't say I am putting them first, before myself."

"Son, I must be direct, perhaps I see something that you do not. If you are not called to the ministry, it would be far better for you to spend your time productively elsewhere. Our seminary is not just a social club, after all. I would advise you to pray earnestly about your choices."

Willie stared at the space in front of him without focusing. "Well, I am relieved in a way. I thought you might have a paddle handy for administering discipline."

"Son, this is not elementary school. I do not think discipline is your problem. Direction is. You need to make a decision with your heart and soul and stick with it. Will you do that for me?"

"Yes sir, I am relieved that you spoke to me. I see you are right, and I will pray for guidance about how to follow my dreams…if I can just get one to sit still!"

Stirrings in Louisville

In 1902, Clyde Buckley invited Willie to speak at his permanent Chautauqua Assembly in Louisville on odd weekends, and asked that he write down stories and lectures in case he was able to join the summer tour. "The pay is good, but the travel is demanding. Not everyone can do it. There are homebodies who just won't travel outside the city limits."

"That's not my way, sir. I have been dreaming about travel, no matter how much I loved being on our farm. My studies at the seminary are not going as well as I hoped, and frankly, the speaking engagements are much more thrilling. With father's new business, I am sure he will permit me to travel."

By the end of the first summer tour, Clyde viewed Willie as one of his rising stars. Always interested in improving his profits, he decided to broach a new subject. "Willie, there is one more possibility that might suit you. You have been writing since childhood, but did you ever publish anything?"

"No sir, except a little poem I wrote that was in a paper in London, England. How that happened is a long story."

"I was thinking more of books. If you will come with me tomorrow, I want to show you the Mayes Printing Company. Here's the thing, if you had books of your talks, you could sell them on the circuit. Here is their address," he said, handing Willie a business card. "Can you meet me there at nine in the morning? I'll drop by today and make sure you can talk to a printer. Bring a sample of your work."

The next day, the two men met with an editor at Mayes Printing Company. Willie had brought along a sheaf of ledger paper with samples of his poems. The editor looked them over and said, "Well, here is the situation. We print all kinds of things here, a lot of it is advertising, and some of it is books. But we are not a publisher that makes its money promoting authors. We can copy edit, we can run off books for people, and bind them either in heavy paper or fine, hardbound bindings. Why, you can even have gold lettering and gold leaf if you want."

"Are you saying that you don't pay the authors for their books? I had not heard of that, how does it work?" Willie asked.

"Say you wanted a hundred copies of your book. We would set the type, run it off and bind it. It would be up to you to sell it yourself, we are not book promoters. But we can keep copies in our warehouse and distribute them when orders arrive."

Clyde smiled. "That's okay, promoting is something we know a bit about. So about what does it cost to print a book with your firm?"

"We can do a paper-back book for about two bits a copy. A hard-bound book might be around a dollar. But you can sell them for twice that and get your money back, if you have a market."

"Thank you for your time," Clyde said. "Well, Willie, that is how it works. I would suggest you put together a book proposal and I can get you started."

"I already have a title," said Willie. "The Road to Success, The Best Little Book in the World."

"Sounds like just the ticket," said the editor. "One thing you will want is a company name to print in the front pages. Do you have any ideas?"

"Sure," said Willie. "The World Supply Company of Louisville, Kentucky. Because we are going to supply the world!"

"That's what I like about you, boy. You never do anything half-way," Clyde said. "Come on, let me buy you lunch!"

William Lee Popham permanently joined Clyde
Buckley's summer Chautauqua circuit in 1905.
Remembering the Dean's admonition, he began
writing fervently. He collected poems, advice, and
anecdotes for a book he presumptuously called
"The Road to Success." Clyde underwrote the cost
of printing 500 copies. "You can leave some at
Mayes Printing," he said, "But do bring a couple
hundred on our tour this summer. You may be
surprised."

The troupe traveled to Washington, D.C. and
Willie got his first look at the Capitol Building and
the Washington Monument. He was now 20 years
old, and flirted with the teen-aged daughter of the
band leader, who had accompanied the group as far
as the capital.

Oddly, the two parted because he refused to kiss
her one evening on the Capitol steps. The moon
was rising over the mall and the fragrance of
honeysuckle wafted in the moonlight. The girl
stepped close to him, took his hand, and admitted
that she was developing feelings for him.

Willie thanked her confusedly, but replied, "I'm
sorry to spoil such an evening, but I feel deeply that
love must come before passion, and love must be
rooted in duty." Embarrassed that he would push
her away, she asked him to escort her back to the
hotel. Leaving his "buts" behind, she departed for
Louisville at the end of the week.

The following day, Willie gave a lecture called
"Can God's Love Defeat the Devil?" Over a
thousand people attended the talk, and Clyde
introduced him as The Boy with the Silver Tongue,

The Plowboy Poet, and The Bard of Kentucky.
Willie's reputation soared, and audiences around
the Southeast began to hear about that wondrous
boy- preacher with a voice like a songbird. Willie
sold all 500 copies from his first printing and wore
out his right hand signing copies at the tent
meetings.

Doing the Trans-Continental

By 1907, William Lee Popham had become a
celebrity on the Kentucky Chautauqua tour, and
Clyde Buckley visited to talk about expanding his
range.

"Willie, you have done a superb job on our
Southern Circuit. I think you are ready for a
national audience. If you are willing to consider
more travel, some of our members will be taking the
train as far as California this summer. There is a
speaking circuit that runs west to Denver, Salt Lake
City, and out to Sacramento. Would you be
interested?"

"Clyde, I would be overjoyed to see the rest of
the United States! California! It's unbelievable!
Just show me the contract!" Willie replied.

"You know that I am a dreamer, night and day,"
Willie continued. "Seeing the grandest mountains
God ever created would feed my dreams. I promise
you, show me the flowers in those mountain valleys
and I will carpet the world with poems!"

From 1907 to 1909, the tour took Willie from
coast to coast and as far north as Niagara Falls. He
engaged in sight-seeing excursions with other

41

speakers that took in the Yosemite Valley in California, Yellowstone National Park in Wyoming, the Black Hills of South Dakota, the Garden of the Gods in Colorado, and Mormon Square in Salt Lake City, Utah.

Willie had ample time to think and write during the train rides between destinations, and he soon hit upon a new formula. He decided to write a basic plot for a romance novel that would take place in each exotic destination. The novel would have a prologue that described the scenery and showed a few photographs to provide a setting for the characters in their ensuing romance. During his travels, he began to write the prologues for books he would complete at home in Louisville in the coming years.

In retrospect, there is little distinction between William Popham's 'Seven Wonders' romances and the advertising brochures he created to describe Saint George Island—except that the characters he was wooing were to become his investors. All that Willie needed to focus his talents was to meet a man who personified success at the turn of the century, and Clyde Buckley was about to make the introduction.

William Jennings Bryan, three-time presidential candidate and the most famous Chautauqua speaker of the Gilded Age.

The Game of Chance

In September, 1909, Clyde Buckley invited Willie to the next Saturday's Chautauqua symposium. "I have a special surprise; you will want to be there the whole afternoon."

"Is it something you can tell me about now?" Willie asked.

"In fact, you need to know because you will be doing the introduction! Yes, I have arranged for William Jennings Bryan to speak."

"*Bryan*," Willie repeated, "You mean the presidential candidate who gave the famous Cross of Gold speech, and just lost the election to President Taft? My word, I *voted* for him! "

43

"Yes sir, the very same man. Come early, the hall will be crowded! I am going to ask Mr. Bryan to speak right after you, if you can keep your remarks brief. Did you know that they used to call him 'The Boy Orator of the Platte'?"

As Clyde had predicted, the hall was crowded in anticipation of hearing the famous man. William Jennings Bryan sat with Clyde in the front row, and Clyde introduced him to Willie. "Mr. Bryan, this young man is Reverend William Lee Popham. You two have quite a bit in common, except that Willie has not yet run for president! Let me introduce him so he can warm up the crowd for you."

After Clyde's introduction, Willie stepped up to the lectern and gestured towards Mr. Bryan. "Tonight, we welcome a very distinguished guest, a man who needs no introduction, as William Jennings Bryan has spoken across the country many times. I am sure many of you voted for him in the last election!" The audience, primarily Southern Democrats, applauded vigorously.

"You all know my reputation for long-winded speeches, and may be afraid that I will lapse into a sermon. Never fear, I would only like to share an anecdote about what is wanted in this country, based on a personal experience from childhood."

"As a boy, I remember sitting beside my favorite brook one day, while the other children were building a dam. They were wading, carrying stones, splashing in the mud and shouting gleefully, but none of them paid any attention to me."

"I began to feel abused and lonely, and was fretting over the neglect, when my Aunt Sally came down the road. "What's the matter, sonny? Why ain't you playing with the rest?"

"They don't want me," I said, digging my fists into my eyes. "They never asked me to come join them." I expected sympathy, but Auntie gave me an impatient push."

"Is that all, you little ninny? Nobody wants folks that'll sit around on a bank and wait to be asked! Run along with the rest and *make yourself wanted*."

"William Jennings Bryan is a man who has made himself wanted without waiting to be asked. He was the first Democrat ever elected to Congress in the Republican state of Nebraska. He stands for temperance, Christian values in the home, and the belief that the women we men love must have the right to vote. His campaigns for President have emphasized the importance of service, prudent use of our national treasure, and solvency. He is truly a man who has made himself wanted, so let's welcome him to the podium to speak for himself!"

The crowd applauded vigorously as Willie shook Mr. Bryan's hand and then sat down next to Clyde.

"Thank you, Reverend Popham, for the kind introduction. Meeting you has reminded me that I always had three ambitions so far back in childhood that I cannot recall when they first arose."

"My first ambition was to be a Baptist preacher. I attended Sunday school faithfully, and whenever anyone asked what I planned to become when I grew up, my answer was the same: A Baptist preacher!"

"Then one day, Father took me to witness a baptism by immersion. I watched the preacher pray over the penitents, and then hold them under water to wash away their sins. Sometimes, the preacher seemed to hold them under for quite a time to be quite sure the believers would become spotless."

"Father," I asked on the way home, "Does a Baptist preacher have to dunk people like that? It seemed more like a drowning."

"Yes, that is how we accept our faith." Father later told me that I never again mentioned a desire to become a Baptist preacher!"

"My second ambition was to become a farmer. Yes, I wanted to have my own pumpkin patch and raise pumpkins. I am sure President Taft and his supporters are glad that I will now have that opportunity without the need to preside over our government!"

"My third ambition was to become a lawyer, and I finally realized that aim. As a boy, I would sit on the courthouse steps and listen to lawyers arguing their cases."

"Later, I studied law and passed the bar. I once played a joke on a friend in college, and we became even closer friends because of it. He is the one who invited me to Nebraska, where I eventually was elected to Congress. And so it is true, I was elected to Congress as a result of a practical joke I played on a friend!"

"One of my colleagues in the House of Representatives made light of my story and said he knew a number of men who were elected to Congress after playing a joke on the whole community!"

"While my ambitions have been changed by circumstance, my ideals of citizenship have not changed. The purpose of what I do, what we all do, is to make this country so great that to be a private citizen of the United States will be greater than to be a king in any other nation!"

"As I have traveled through this country, I have met young men, sons of farmers, sons of merchants, or professional men, who have one ideal in common. Namely, they have been preparing for service. Often they do not know just what line of work they would follow, but they have been preparing for service so that they may rise to greatness when the opportunity arises!"

"I mention ideals rather than money. For if a young man asks me how he can make a fortune in a day, I cannot tell him. If he asks how he can become rich in a year, I know not what to answer. But I can tell him that if he will locate in any community and live an honest life, a useful life, an industrious life, he will make friends who are fastened to him with bonds of steel. And before much time has passed, his fellows will call on him to represent them in important matters, and help govern the community. This is the service for which our young people must prepare, so that our country may remain great and not fall prey to moneyed interests and elitists."

"There is far too much interest in money. In the last election, I learned that the other party was buying votes, and was approached by a farmer who said that he would be glad to vote for me for a dollar! Members of my own party thought it wise to pay, and said that it was 'fighting the devil with fire.' But I disagree. It is poor policy to fight the devil with fire. He knows more about the subject than we do, and does not have to pay for his fuel!"

After William Jennings Bryan's speech, Willie approached him. "Sir, I very much enjoyed your thoughts on service, and admit to having had the same ambitions to become a preacher or a farmer— though pumpkins never crossed my mind! But you changed your goals, and I take it you are not practicing law now. Would you think it rude if I asked how you support your family?"

"Not at all, son. I have given as many as 500 speeches a year on the Chautauqua Circuit. During my last presidential campaign, I once gave 15 speeches in 18 hours! I also have a newspaper, *The Commoner*, and together the income quite suffices."

As Willie left the hall, he spoke briefly to Clyde. "Between you, Mr. Bryan, and the Dean at college, I am seeing a new path open. I have not written a book since 1905. It is time for a change!"

Maude Miller Estes, Authoress

"Love Poems and the Boyhood

Of Kentucky's Poet"

Louisville, Kentucky circa 1910

Meeting Maude

Hearing William Jennings Bryan speak crystallized Willie's goals. Here was a man who had become wealthy through service, oratorical genius, deep Christian faith, and artful use of the printed word.

In October, 1909, Willie began writing a series of books of poems and short romances. No longer hampered by lack of funds, he turned out "Love's Rainbow Dream," "She Dared to Win," "The Valley of Love," "Village by the Sea" and "A Tramp's Love" during the first half of 1910. Each book was about 60 pages long and sold for 50 cents. Each featured a hero who either won a fair lady, or failed at romance and was forced to learn hard lessons about courtly love.

Not stopping with fiction, Willie turned to his stock of poems, advice and sermons. He published "Silver Gems in Seas of Gold," a compilation of his writings, poems, anecdotes and lectures. "Nutshells of Truth" was a brief collection of toasts and aphorisms. Finally, he compiled "Poems of Truth, Love and Power." Because he owned the copyright to every book, he freely lifted poems and passages and republished them under a new title.

Starting in 1911, Willie began writing short novels that he liked to call the Seven Wonders of the World Romances. In every case, a handsome young traveler meets a winsome and moral young lady whose father obstinately objects to their relationship. In every case, the girl's kid brother falls into the raging torrent, slips at the edge of a cliff, or dangles over the depths of a cave—only to be pulled to safety by the gallant traveler. Relenting, the father shakes his hand and offers his daughter in marriage.

Young William's fancy had always focused on thoughts of love—but now his thoughts had grown serious. He had written 16 books about romantic love in two years. The loneliness of his railroad tours nagged him, and he wondered if he would ever meet a suitable bride.

One evening after Willie gave a lecture on "Lovers in the Garden of Eden" at the Louisville Chautauqua Assembly, Clyde introduced him to a young woman named Maude Miller Estes. She was an outgoing, pert young woman with a sense of style, notwithstanding her pence nez glasses.

"Reverend Popham, Miss Estes is among your admirers. She frequently attends our meetings, and she and I have done some conspiring behind your back. She has suggested that she write your biography."

"I am very glad to meet you," said William Lee approvingly. "But I am only 25 years old. Why would anyone want to write a biography of me? I don't understand."

"Let me answer," Miss Estes replied, "Firstly, you are a remarkable speaker, and have quite a reputation despite your age. People do wonder how you developed your talents. Secondly, Mr. Buckley tells me that you have published 16 books in just two years! Is that the case?"

"Well, that is all true," said Willie. "Words, phrases and scenes just appear in my mind as I travel and daydream and I feel compelled to write them down. Ever since childhood, I have always kept papers with my poems, lectures and stories."

"I can envision the two of you working together," said Clyde. "Now if you'll excuse me, I have to make sure the hall gets cleaned up for tomorrow."

51

"You can call me Maude, and I would truly enjoy the chance to work on a project with you," Miss Estes said to William Lee.

"I go by Willie to my friends," he replied. With cheeks blushing, he added "I would like to think of you as my friend. And I would be happy to show you my work."

For the next six months, Maude gathered Willie's poems and interspersed them with stories from his boyhood, observations about his piety and love of Womanhood. She published "Love Poems and the Boyhood of Kentucky's Poet" in the fall of 1910 through the Mayes Printing Company. His photograph was captioned, "EVANGELIST, AUTHOR, LECTURER, POET."

Willie and Maude kept up their correspondence after her book was published. He had come to love her with the same kind of devotion he felt towards his mother, but mixed with pangs of intimate attraction. Willie continued traveling and speaking, but his frequent travels were leaving him feeling uprooted. Impetuously, Willie wrote to Maude during his 1912 lecture tour to Georgia, proposing marriage.

"Dearest Maude, I am ashamed to confess that whenever I give a talk, the ladies approach me in an almost indecent way. Their behavior makes it difficult for a principled man to travel the way I do. You may think this too sudden, but you are by far my closest lady friend. In our work together, I have come to love you and wonder if you feel that way towards me? Let me jump off the cliff. Would you consider marrying me? If the answer is yes, I expect to be in McDonough, Georgia next week. May I request an answer most urgently? Whether you say yea or nay, let's keep this proposal our secret for now."

Maude did not hesitate, and took a train from Louisville to McDonough, Georgia where the two sweethearts were married by the Henry County judge on May 11, 1912. The decision was so sudden that no family had been invited. The couple decided it would be funny and romantic to keep their marriage a secret from Clyde and the other traveling speakers for a few weeks.

A typical poem promoting Florida by William Lee Popham, here used as a caption for a post card.

Intermission. Was there Sex on the Beach?

Let's take an interlude from William Popham's frenzied beginnings en route to Apalachicola, where he would try to combine oystering with real estate sales. To adopt a modern perspective, Saint George Island has been regarded as a place for lovers' trysts as long as people have lived on Apalachicola Bay. Mores and social norms are best left on the mainland. As one raconteur recently explained, "You know what Islanders call that land north of the bridge? The U-nited States."

Loggerhead turtles may have started the trend of arriving annually under the spring tides of a full moon "solely for the purpose of reproduction." College kids on Spring Break, newlyweds who marry in the State Park, and honeymooners gladly continue the tradition.

For men, the unofficial motto of Saint George Island is, "First buy the beer, then find the bait, then hit the beach." Lady visitors tend to substitute, "Buy the bikini, bring a book, and hit the beach." They may choose a chilled white wine instead of beer, preferably *Far Niente*. At any rate, mixing men, women, bikinis and spirituous beverages with summer sun has predictable results.

My brother-in-law can confirm that a spirit of devilishness inhabits Saint George Island. One moonless midnight, he was walking Meg, his long-legged black Labrador field dog, on the beach when she ran off into the darkness. Puzzled, he turned on his flashlight, only to behold three separate couples

54

running naked down the beach. "By my flashlight, I could confirm that they were anatomically male and female in equal numbers."

As Meg "greeted" the first girl with her big, wet nose, the girl screamed, "Doggy! Doggy! BLACK Doggy!" The second couple dove into the water (possibly not aware that sharks cruise the beaches at night), while the third couple scrambled under a catamaran parked on the beach, where they had hidden their clothes.

Meg did not miss the opportunity to introduce herself in the friendly manner of all Labrador retrievers. Whatever the third girl screamed out was not completely audible, but my brother-in-law interpreted it as a wish for atonement and a promise never again to undertake "what Mamma don't allow."

Spend some time on Saint George Island, and your fancy assuredly will turn to thoughts of love. There used to be a big bull 'gator in a pond up in the State Park, then one spring it was gone. I asked a Park Ranger if they had removed it. "No," he said, "That old 'gator has gone 'gal-ing.'" Gators have been known to swim across four miles of shark-infested salt water just for one amorous opportunity.

To paraphrase Cole Porter, "Oysters in the bay, 'gainst their wish, do it, Even lazy jellyfish- do it, Let's do it, let's fall in love." That said, a friend of mine is dubious about the reputation of oysters for intimate prowess. "I had a dozen the other day in Apalachicola. Only the first nine worked."

55

William Lee Popham had the motivation, the opportunity, and the means to participate in Sex on the Beach, but did he ever follow through? As a Baptist preacher, he abstained from all alcoholic beverages. Strike one. He also refrained from dancing, even though his wife enjoyed it. He is reputed to have hired townsmen to escort Maude to various dances. Strike two. There is no evidence that the couple ever actually spent the night on Saint George Island. Moreover, the Pophams were in Jacksonville when their only child was conceived in March, 1917. Strike three. We may conclude that the man who bought Saint George Island never did have Sex on the Beach.

He may be the only adult visitor of any animal species who is able to make this claim. A word of warning, however, to those who might be inspired by these anecdotes: Bring your bug spray, because gnats, mosquitoes and those biting yellow flies of August are also planning to have Sex on the Beach!

"It's amazing! They come here exactly the same week every year, and solely for the purpose of reproduction!"

Act III. From Preacher and Poet to 'Oyster King'

"It was a bold man who ate the first oyster!"

-Jonathan Swift

An Interrupted Honeymoon

As Willie and Maude were leaving the Atlanta suburbs after their wedding, he asked, "Sweetheart, the Chautauqua Company toured Florida last year and it was grand to see the land of oranges and orchids. Have you ever traveled there?"

"No, Willie, I have never been that far south. I had to earn a living in Louisville and never had the resources to travel-- and of course, a lady requires a companion for such adventures!"

"Well, you simply must see it! How about if we honeymoon there as soon as I finish my lectures in Atlanta?" Maude agreed and their plans were set in motion. Their first stop was the Terminal Hotel in Atlanta, where Clyde had booked the company for an appearance.

"No one knows we are married, so we will need to book separate rooms if we want to keep this a secret," Willie told Maude. It did not seem to be a problem because the couple had not yet learned to share their lives. They checked in separately and got keys for two rooms on the same floor.

As the bellman helped them move their luggage to the room, Maude changed her mind. She whispered to her husband, "After all, we are married. I don't really see the point in staying apart from you after waiting for two years." Over supper, they agreed to stay together in one room.

Early the next morning, there was a loud and unexpected knock on their door. Willie opened the door to find a surly looking, uniformed watchman who pushed into the room. "Sir, this hotel is a fine establishment that does not tolerate indecency. I don't care who you are, you can't cohabit with an unmarried woman. I have reported you to the Atlanta police and must request that you both come with me to the station for an interview."

Willie and Maude were stunned and immediately protested. Maude told the watchman, "Sir, besides being insolent, you are completely wrong!"

"Lady, that is not what you said when you checked in. We don't put up with this kind of thing, now get your coat and come along!"

At the police station, Willie was charged with illicitly entering a lady's room and the pair was brought before a judge. Still wishing to keep their marriage a secret, they asked how much the bond would be. When they learned it was six dollars apiece, they decided to pay it and leave for their Florida honeymoon.

On the train, Willie purchased a copy of the Atlanta *Journal*, and was horrified to see the headline on the society page: "Preacher and Author Found in Lady's Room at Terminal Hotel!"

"This is getting worse, now it sounds as if there were three of us!" They disembarked at the first stop, purchased return tickets, and registered again at the Terminal Hotel. Willie summoned reporters and explained what they had meant to be a joke, this time producing their marriage license. He requested and received a retraction in the next edition. Relieved that their reputations had been salvaged, they finally told Clyde of their wedding and change in plans. Willie and Maude caught the next day's train to Florida.

'Willie, I certainly hope this last week does not foreshadow our life together. I have never experienced so much emotional tumult."

"I felt that way at the time, but now that it is over, it was quite a thrill, don't you think, Dear? Don't you worry about a thing; we are in Our Savior's hip pocket!"

Maude turned to stare out the window. "Listen to yourself, Willie, offering nothing but cold comfort. You know Jesus did not even have a hip pocket!"

"Now, Maude, let's kiss and make up. We can do it, we're married, you know?"

"All right, but from now on, I am going to call you Wicked Willie! For a preacher, you are such a tease!"

If Once You Saw This Place, You Would Buy It!

On their honeymoon, Willie and Maude took the train from Atlanta to Jacksonville. After hearing that beaches were much finer on the Gulf Coast, they crossed the state on the Seaboard Line to Tampa and Clearwater Beach. It was there that they met James Abbott, a Tampa real estate developer. Willie wrote to Clyde Buckley and told him he would be leaving the Chautauqua Circuit because he and Maude had decided to live in Tampa and work with James Abbott's real estate firm.

James quickly noted Willie's talent for writing. Soon, Willie was writing all their advertising copy in his inimitable way, combining poetry with photographs and florid descriptions of the area's potential for guaranteed happiness and profits. The couple lived happily at their home on the banks of the Alafia River.

One afternoon in 1916, Willie asked James about his favorite vacation spots in Florida. James paused and smiled. "Southwest of Tallahassee, there is a town called Apalachicola. The town is located where a river enters the bay. Apalachicola means, "the people on the other side", namely, the west side of the bay."

"From Apalach, you can take a boat to a place called St. George's Island. It is almost thirty miles of white sand beaches, just one ten-room hotel, and a lighthouse. Don't let me spoil it for you, but if once you saw it, you would buy it!"

"You mean you saw it but did not buy it yourself? How come?"

"Because Capital City Bank of Tallahassee owns it, and when Cecilia and I visited back in 1914, they weren't selling. But I have heard they might want to turn it loose, so why don't you and Maude go see for yourselves. You won't be disappointed!"

With James' blessings, Willie and Maude booked a Seaboard Railway ticket to Tallahassee in September of 1916. They stayed there a few days while Willie visited the Capital City Bank and was directed to George Saxon, who had originally purchased the island.

Willie told Mr. Saxon that he was an author, lecturer and real estate agent from the Tampa area, and wanted to visit Apalachicola and see St. George Island. "Oh, certainly, I can arrange that. Let me give you some names of contacts in Apalachicola who can show you around."

"Incidentally," Mr. Saxon continued, "Apalachicola is on the west bank of the river, and there is no simple way of getting there by highway. By far the most scenic route is to book railway tickets to Carrabelle, and ferry over to town on the Crescent City steamer. The railroad is the Georgia, Florida and Alabama Line, but we joke that the initials stand for 'Gophers, Frogs and Alligators!' Which is not too far off the mark, by the way."

"Okay, we will book tickets in the morning. It would be kind of you to give us some contacts," Willie replied. "I have heard that you have business interests there, how are they progressing?"

"Oh, yes, my main business is cypress lumber. I acquired a sawmill and there is a good demand for black cypress in particular. But the island has disappointed me. I thought we could do a brisk business to the hotel, but it has not happened. Most people in Tallahassee don't even know the island exists. Frankly, the bank needs to find a better developer, or else just sell the island. Our income never offsets our expenses, to tell the truth."

Willie said good-bye, pleased to have several people to contact in Apalachicola. He booked two tickets on the Georgia, Florida and Alabama railroad spur. They boarded the next morning for a two-hour ride to Carrabelle on 'The Moonlight Express.'

Moonlight Express to the Gulf

All people along the line to Lanark Village may enjoy a dip in the brine and drink in the salt air of the Gulf of Mexico. Supper will be served at the luxurious Lanark Inn after your bath or sail, and a NEW CASINO affords entertainment. Remember the day, the hour, and the low excursion fare!

Entering Apalachicola

The engineer blew the steam whistle as the little train reached Lanark Village east of Carrabelle. The Gulf of Mexico came into view, and Maude and Willie looked out on Apalachicola Bay for the first time. The train stopped at a small clapboard depot, and two vacationing families from Georgia disembarked at Lanark.

Half an hour later, the train passed a large lumber yard and pulled into the depot at Carrabelle. Docks were visible along the river, with a number of seagoing boats tied up at the piers. The *Crescent City*, a beautiful side-wheeler, was berthed next to the train depot. Its route was timed to receive passengers from the train and ferry them westward. The Pophams bought tickets to Apalachicola and boarded the steam-powered paddle wheeler.

As the steamboat pulled out of the Carrabelle River mouth, Willie looked across Apalachicola Bay and saw a dark green line of trees rising above a low elevation, extending as far to the west as he could see. "Look, Maude, there it is! St. George Island, Florida! Tomorrow, we will take a launch across and visit her for the first time." The Crescent City docked in Eastpoint for half an hour and then ferried across Apalachicola Bay.

The ferry dock was only one block from the Franklin Hotel, and the couple checked in for an indefinite stay. As soon as they obtained room keys, Willie asked the clerk how to get over to the island. "There is a motor launch that goes over every few days, but George Summit turpentines on the island, I imagine he would show you around for a few bucks. Let me give him a call for you and set it up."

The clerk reached for a candlestick telephone and called the exchange. After a few moments of talking, he reported, "George can take you over in the morning after breakfast. He'll stop by and escort you to his boat, he docks where Avenue G meets Water Street."

Willie tipped the clerk for his trouble and grinned at Maude. "Isn't progress wonderful! I am impressed that they have electricity and a telephone exchange way out here already. "

THE STEAMER, *CRESCENT CITY*, AT THE DOCKS IN APALACHICOLA, FLORIDA.

Seven years after the Popham's first visit, Anne and Mary Ellen Gibson purchased the Franklin Hotel and renamed it the Gibson Inn. To this day, the veranda remains a popular gathering place for townspeople who enjoy 'Happy Hour' and live music.

First Look, Saint George Island

The next morning, Willie and Maude dressed in khaki outfits and hiking shoes before going to breakfast. As they were finishing, the morning clerk entered and introduced them to George Summit, a small, wiry man with callused hands and a swarthy, deeply lined face. "If you're ready to go, I can take you right now. For a dollar a head, I can show you around. The turpentine can wait a day."

George led them two blocks down the street and turned towards the docks. He helped them climb down a ladder into his 18-foot, open skiff. "I hope you don't mind, but it's a working boat. Reckon it will take half an hour to get over to Nick's Hole."

The passengers were both unsteady in the rocking boat. "Just sit down, I will cast off. Do it every day by myself." He untied the bow line from its cleat and got in. "I got the first outboard motor in town; everyone else is still using sails or steam to get around. Hold on now."

George primed the engine and pulled the starter rope several times before the engine fired. He put the engine in forward gear and eased out into the smooth river current. "Hold onto your hats," he joked. George guided the boat past a bank of sand bars in the river mouth and then turned slightly southeast, heading for the middle of the island. To the east, Willie could see a small fleet of oyster boats with sails furled while men stood on sideboards along the gunwales, vigorously working long-handled oyster rakes.

"George, did you ever try your hand at that," Willie shouted, pointing at the oyster fleet.

"Yes, I've done it. Every man and boy in Apalachicola knows how to tong," he replied. "Pay is good in a good year, and being on the bay can get in your blood. But you have to work 'from can to cain't'. Hit a few years of drought, floods, or storms and you can't feed your family on it."

"Look ahead of us, that's the dock at Nick's Hole. I'll keep the boat between the markers and tie up so we can go to the hotel." George slowed the boat and turned so the bow faced open water, then tied bow and stern lines to iron cleats on the dock. He jumped onto the dock and helped his passengers clamber up a wooden ladder.

"Ladies and Gentlemen, Saint George Island awaits you!" For another dollar, you can get lunch and something to drink at the hotel. They always have a few guests this time of year, but they would be down on the beach."

Behind them, Apalachicola could be seen as a few tiny buildings on a point of land four miles across the bay, which was sparkling with sails of oystermen who had finished their work and were heading home. The dock ended at a boardwalk that led past saw grass and sedge into a pine woods. Mockingbirds and cardinals flitted through orange-berried Yaupon holly bushes along the boardwalk, while pelicans and gulls flew overhead. A fresh breeze blew towards them from the Gulf side of the island.

"How far it is it over to the hotel?" asked Maude. "'Bout a pistol shot," replied George. "Most places, you can see the bay and the Gulf at the same time." Just as he said that, the boardwalk reached a high point where the tall longleaf pines gave way to much lower scrub oak. The hotel, a two-story wood

**The boardwalk across Saint George Island
with the 'Club House' at left much as William
and Maude Popham first saw it in 1916. The
Gulf of Mexico is visible in the distance past the
hotel.**

frame building that badly needed painting, could be
seen two hundred yards ahead.

"The hotel sits on dunes at the highest part of the
island," George noted as they arrived. "During the
Civil War, the Yankees blockaded the town and
used the island for picnics and recreation. Some
people still call Nick's Hole "Yankee Cove"
because a schooner was positioned there to watch
for blockade runners coming out the river mouth."

From the hotel, the boardwalk continued over the
dunes past waving sea oats and beach verbena, then
down wooden stairs to the beach. A four-room bath
house stood next to the end of the walkway and

tracks could be seen going to the beach where four guests had their pick of a dozen wooden lounge chairs arrayed under blue umbrellas.

"Let's go in the hotel and I will introduce you to the staff, in case you have any questions." Inside, a balding man wearing a red vest greeted them. "Hello, George, who have you brought over today?"

"This is Mr. and Mrs. William and Maude Popham," he replied.

"Will you be staying with us? I don't see any luggage."

"No, we have been dying to see Saint George Island since we heard about it down in Tampa where we live," Willie replied. "George Saxon put us in touch with some businessmen and suggested we stay in town at the Franklin."

"Mr. Saxon is my employer. So are you here on business or pleasure?"

"A little of both," said Willie. "Is your dining room open? After we take a look at the beach, we could stop for a bite and explain. First, though, we need to see the beach, I have been dreaming about it for a month."

George led them down to the bathhouse and they greeted the hotel guests, each of whom was wearing swim wear. There were four adults watching a young girl and boy playing by the shore. "Where are you folks from, and what do you think of Saint George Island?" Willie asked.

"Tallahassee, we came down on the train and took the steam launch across," replied a tall, tanned gentleman. "What do we think? Best spot to relax in the state of Florida! Just look at that surf!" His wife nodded in agreement. "The children love it too; it is hard to get them to leave. I hate to think about it, but our stay is up tomorrow."

"There is no place with beaches and surf like this for hundreds of miles. Saint Vincent's Island is privately owned and the beaches are flat and hard. The bay is shallow and has no surf, it's more like a lake, and most places, the shore is saw grass and sedge. Dog Island off Carrabelle is much smaller, and the next island, Cedar Key, is a hundred miles away. If you go west, there are sand spits but no islands. Snow-white sand and island surf are why we come to Saint George."

Willie turned to Maude with a wistful look and spoke quietly to her. "Do you know what I would love to do more than anything else I can think of?"

Maude looked at her husband, seeming a bit puzzled. "No, I can't guess. What are you contemplating?"

"I would relish being able to share this place. So many people are stuck at their work in cities now; they don't get to enjoy nature the way I did growing up. But things are changing very fast. A few years ago, there was no railroad here. Now that there are automobiles, there will need to be bridges for highways along the coast. The Gulf Coast is going to open up, and soon. If other people saw Saint George Island, they would love it too. There _will_ be a bridge to Saint George Island before you know it!"

Willie turned to George again. "How big is this island, George?"

"If you count Little Saint George, it is 26 miles long. That is really the same island, but the hurricane of '99 cut a channel through. Filled in again, but people still call it Little Saint George. The old lighthouse is over there on the seaward Cape not far from West Pass, across from Saint Vincent's."

One of the women pointed towards the Gulf, "Oh, look, dolphins, just past the sandbar!" One of the dolphins slapped the water with its fluke, sending spray skyward. Two pelicans flew over the pod and dove on the mullet the dolphins were chasing.

"Doesn't that beat all?" Willie said. "So the island is twenty-six miles long, and how many people live here?"

"Just two families, really--the lighthouse keeper on Cape Saint George, and his helper. Plus they hired a schoolteacher for their children. Other than that, it's the Club House staff and a turpentine camp."

"It would be fun to loll around the beach, but Maude and I really want to see more of the island. Shall we go back to the hotel for refreshments? Folks, thanks for pointing out the porpoises, it has been a treat!"

After ordering sandwiches and iced tea at the hotel, the three visitors walked back to the boat. "What else can you show us, George?"

"We are not quite in the middle of the island, with my little boat, the best thing is to head towards Little Saint George. If you don't mind, I need to talk to the foreman of my turpentine operation too. If we went east, it would be too far to get back to Apalach."

George pointed to a finger of land to the east. "That is Cedar Point. From there, it is still more than ten miles to East Pass." He started the boat and turned westward.

The Ancient Ones

George motored along for half an hour until a second dock came into view in a shallow bay. As they arrived, a great blue heron squawked and flew ahead to a shallow bar where two brilliant white egrets were already wading. George tied up the boat and helped Willie and Maude out of the boat.

"My crew is turpentining up in the pines," George said. "Take a look around while I go talk to the foreman. This is the widest part of the island, and it is over a mile to the lighthouse, I don't suggest walking over there without plenty of drinking water."

Maude and Willie stepped off the pier and walked along the bay shore while George went to check on his turpentine crew. Marsh wrens flitted in and out of the wire grass that grew in patches along the bay, interspersed with sandy areas. Maude noticed that bayside sand appeared tea-stained compared to the white 'sugar sand' on the Gulf beaches, and looked at hermit crabs scuttling along a few feet from shore. Where waves washed up on the beach, she noticed dark, irregular pieces that did not seem to be shells.

"Willie, what are those shapes that are washing up along the tide line?" He bent down and picked up a few of the larger objects, then washed them free of sand and algae.

"Would you look at these!" he exclaimed. "They look like broken pottery!" He gave them to Maude as they walked along, noticing some larger pieces.

"There is one that seems to have a design," Maude pointed out. As they waited for George to return, they found a few shards decorated with lines, rope marks, points and whorls. Willie rinsed them off and put them in a handkerchief.

When George returned, they showed him their find. "What do you know about these, George?"

"Oh yes, if you spend any time on the island, you find Indian artifacts. When Apalachicola was founded, there were Indians living along the bay on Saint Vincent's Island, that is why they named the area Indian Pass."

"So these could be a hundred years old?" asked Maude.

"There is no way to know, they could be much older. People who study these things say the Indians have lived here for over a thousand years.

Ancient, incised pottery sherd and shell midden from the barrier islands in Apalachicola Bay.

Some of them would go up to the high land around Tallahassee in the summer and come down here to gather shellfish and fin fish in the winter."

George pointed across West Pass toward Saint Vincent Island. "Along the bay over there, you will find deep piles of shell with pines or palm trees growing right through them. Must have taken a long time to eat that many oysters. Seems as if they stayed in the shelter of the trees on the bay where the food was, you don't find shell mounds along the Gulf."

Willie was inspired. "There is just no end of surprises on Saint George Island! George, we have seen enough. If you are done with your business, let's head back to Apalachicola!"

They thanked George for an amazing day on the water and walked back to the Franklin Hotel. That evening, Willie and Maude studied the pottery in wonderment. Willie felt compelled to express himself and got out his writing paper. With the pottery bits as his muse, he wrote and rewrote a poem.

When Seas Shift Middens

Their waves washed ashore, not tinted sea-green;
Their combers were not colored in 'aquamarine.'
Their sounds were not like ours, their sky was not 'blue;'
Who knows what their elders called sapphire hue?
What words did they cry out when storm-clouds unfurled,
To ward away danger blowing into their world?
When pelicans dove into waves after fish,
Did daughters carve shapes on each newly turned dish?
Was there meaning in whorls decorating their clay,
Like cries of sea-eagles searching over the bay?

Now oysters attach to the ancient ones' middens,
Where hermit crabs scuttle o'er pots shattered and hidden,
Shards buried in sands that shine whiter than time,
Clean-scoured by waves from traces of rime.
I turn a fired fragment in the palm of my hand,
Not thinking what they thought, for I don't understand--
To me, it's charred clay that washed up from Gulf bars--
But they cooked sacred food once in maps of their stars.
I turn back to the landing facing into salt-wind...
Thinking someone might be watching, someone might be kin.

Buying Saint George Island

On the way back to Tampa, William and Maude Popham stopped in Tallahassee to talk to George Saxon again. "People tell me you might be interested in selling Saint George Island, is that the case?

George was puffing on a cigar. He put it in an ash tray, ruffled his red hair, and replied, "Yes, it has not worked out the way my associates and I planned. It is hard to get to, and only a few people in Tallahassee have wanted to buy in."

"That is unfortunate, but I can tell you, I am interested and would like to talk about it. How much would you be asking?" Willie replied.

"Capital City Bank would like to get $30,000 out of it," Mr. Saxon replied.

"I can raise some cash, probably not that much," Willie said. "But Maude and I are authors. Besides our real estate, we have probably $10,000 equity in our published books. Would you consider taking the publishing rights as down payment and let us work on developing the island?," Willie asked.

George pondered the offer. "As far as an arrangement, it would be possible to take a down payment and arrange a mortgage for the rest. I could make you the agent for the island if you would agree to set up an account with our bank for any proceeds you might earn. By the way, what kind of books are we talking about?"

Willie grinned. "Love, romance, travel and poetry books. There are over a dozen, with seven in my travel romance series, like *Yosemite Valley Romance* and *Washington Monument Romance*."

"I wouldn't know anything about romance novels," replied Mr. Saxon. "Can you give me contact information for your publisher?"

Willie pulled out a business card with the address for World Supply Company and handed it to Mr. Saxon. "These folks will assure you what our books are worth. The books have sold well; I intentionally combined exotic travel destinations with the triumph of love."

They shook hands and agreed that William Lee could try his hand at selling lots on the island, and would take full possession after Capital City Bank settled its rights to the deed and wrote the mortgage.

On the train to Tampa, Willie hugged his wife elatedly. "Maude, you and I are in God's hip pocket. Saint George Island is not about turpentine and hogs, it is about romance and poetry. It takes a dreamer to see it."

In his mind, he was already composing poems about the joys of living on Saint George Island.

At about the same time, George Saxon was scratching his head. "Romance novels as equity? What the devil was I thinking? I better give that publishing company a call." He was neither the first nor the last businessman to ask that question.

First Baptist Church in Apalachicola where William Popham gave several sermons and was once asked to become minister. Until 1934, it was called Calvary Baptist Church. The tower originally supported a tall steeple.

Apalachicola Sermon

During their trip to Saint George Island, the Pophams had attended Sunday services at Calvary Baptist Church in Apalachicola and also visited the Methodist Church. During their chat, the Methodist minister asked if William was the same Popham who spoke on the Chautauqua circuit. "Yes sir, I am that man. I can present lectures or sermons. I studied at the Southern Baptist Theological Seminary in Louisville, but was never ordained."

"I thought I had heard of you before, and just wanted to be sure. Please let me know when you next return. Perhaps you could speak to our congregation? That would let you meet some of our citizens, and they could get to know you."

"I would be delighted!" replied William Lee. "Would January be too soon?" And so it was Reverend W.T. Brantley who invited William Lee Popham to the pulpit and introduced the future 'Oyster King' to the citizens of Apalachicola.

In January, the Pophams returned from Tampa to Apalachicola as promised, and booked a room at the Franklin Hotel. When the Sunday of Willie's sermon arrived, the couple made their way to the Methodist Church. Reverend Brantley gave a brief introduction, explained that William Popham was an evangelist who had spoken on the Chautauqua circuit for years, and invited him to the pulpit. William put on his "evangelist hat," thanked his host, and turned to the congregation.

"Brothers and Sisters, greetings! Maude and I are delighted to be in Apalachicola, and cannot express how pleased we are to be invited to your church. We plan to move to Apalachicola soon, and make it our home. Both of us hope to meet and work with every one of you to promote business here.

You all know the text I have chosen by heart: 'For God so loved the world that He gave his only begotten Son, that whosoever believeth in Him should not perish, but have everlasting life.' John 3:16 is the core of our faith, but let us go into the great mystery of Love and think of how it guides our lives.

Willie smiled broadly at the congregation. "People who know me soon realize that there is no

subject I would rather talk about than love.
Shouldn't we always do our best to *love* our way
through the world? To love our enemies, that they
may become friends? Love never has never failed
and never will fail."

A number of people in the congregation nodded
agreement and returned Willie's smile.

"'God is love;' and His love will ever guide us. I
have tried to express this in a poem, *Love Will
Guide You*, if I may recite it now that I hold you
captive!" He declaimed,

> Tho' the road be rugged
> O'er grief's benighted way,
> The star of love will guide you
> To a purer, fairer day.
> For the soul of man enlarges
> And the heart forgets its pain
> When life to love surrenders
> Letting only peace remain.
> Free thy soul from every idle!
> And the love which fear defied
> Will put to flight all evil
> And conquer selfish pride.
> Love will "burn the bridges"
> Across the stream of woe
> Leaving far behind you
> Each evil-minded foe.
> If your way is rugged,
> And the stones have tried you so.
> Crowns of peace are waiting
> Where love will ever guide you.
> If the road is rugged
> Be thou not resigned,

For future's way is brighter
Than the fairest way behind.

"And where is it that we first learn of Love and
of Our Savior's message of Redemption? It is at
home, where our Mother's love envelopes us. The
sweetest flower that blooms on the tree of human
life is a mother's love. The gentle hand that rocks
the cradle in childhood's happy dream is the hand
that rules the world."

Willie paused and reflected, "I usually find that
the ladies understand and welcome this message.
Of course, men must express their love in different
ways, we must toil at our businesses and our daily
labors. And yet, even in that work, love must guide
us. For the gentlemen in the congregation, I would
share these thoughts in another verse:"

"Don't say that the world is evil
And every one's out for the money;
Don't mimic the goal of the buzzard
But the bee that seeks the honey:
For life is a withering blossom
Containing the bitter and the sweet;
And its fruit will ripen in heaven
If we stay at the Savior's feet.

In the tender heart of the rosebud
Is sleeping a beautiful rose;
So in the heart of each man
Doth the flower of goodness repose.
And to awaken the flower,
You must be patient and kind
Seeing not the evil prevailing,
For 'tis often wise to be blind.

The Savior "came not to condemn";
Nor merely to reform,
But stood upon the sea
And calmed the raging storm.
Not to condemn, but to redeem
Was the Savior's glad-hearted mission
Calming the storm in sinners' hearts
In their troubled condition.
And if the storm of trouble
In your own heart is abiding.
Remember, in the shadows of night
A beautiful star is hiding."

"There are a hundred other ways love touches us each day, from the pleasant hellos we exchange on the street to the lessons our teachers strive to impart. Our Savior's Love carries us through the troubles of the day and reveals the beauties of the morning sky, the quiet river, and the tumbling surf."

"In this spirit, Maude and I look forward to meeting every one of you, and welcome the happy chance to call you our friends as we come to live in Apalachicola! Amen!"

The congregation loudly repeated, "Amen!", and Willie asked, "Now, Reverend Whatley, won't you please come up and reclaim your pulpit!"

Reverend Whatley led the congregation in a prayer of thanks, and discussed a few upcoming church events that were noted in the bulletin.

"There will be a reception for William and Maude after the service, so please join us there," the Reverend said as he asked the organist to play a recessional. After saying their good-byes to people leaving the church, Reverend Whatley led Maude and Willie to the reception area next to the church kitchen.

After a few minutes of circulating among church members, a tall, striking woman with a streak of white through her brunette hair approached the Pophams. "Hello, I am Mrs. Helen Brooks Smith, actually of Lakeland," she said, greeting Reverend Whatley, William and Maude in turn. "What a sermon, so filled with poetry! I absolutely loved your inspiring message!"

After some small talk, she told William quietly that she had heard he was purchasing Saint George Island, and that she was secretary for an investment group. "If we could meet, I would like to talk to you about the future of Saint George Island." Helen handed Willie her card and told him she would be staying at the Franklin Hotel for another week.

"Excellent, Maude and I are also at the Franklin! We can visit tomorrow if you like!"

The Saint George Company

William Popham met with Helen Brooks Smith on Monday morning and was introduced to her business partner, John Malcolmson, a tall Canadian who sported a goatee.

"Friends call me Captain John, and I am treasurer of our group. We have formed the Saint George Company in Lakeland for the purpose of developing the island. Honestly, it was a shock to

83

us to learn that George Saxon had already
negotiated an agreement with you."

"Nevertheless, we are particularly interested in
that island hotel," John stated. "I have managed
two successful hotels in Canada and it would be no
trouble to get on my feet in the States. So if you
can see a way to work together, let's talk about it."

"Yes, I have an agreement to sell properties on
Saint George Island through George Saxon and
Capital City Bank," Willie replied. "Based on the
amount you have raised, I can offer you one
thousand acres centered around the hotel with rights
to use the boardwalk. If you agree, I would ask for
a $500 deposit and monthly payments of $250
towards a full purchase price of ten thousand
dollars. Then you will have title to the land and
can sell lots, run the hotel, and develop your
investment."

Mrs. Smith and Captain John agreed, took over
the Club House, and renamed it "The Breakers." It
was no coincidence that they copied the name of
Henry Flagler's famous East Coast resort in Palm
Beach, which he built as a destination for travelers
on his railroad from New York. The Lakeland
group purchased a 32 foot motor launch, also
named *The Breakers,* to transport prospective
clients to the island, and began to advertise in the
Lakeland and Tampa area.

Popham thought their plan was excellent, and
prepared an illustrated, 36 page pamphlet extolling
Saint George Island to advertise their business. He
also started a new firm called The Saint George
Island Company with his Tampa associates,

intending to develop his portion by selling tracts to other developers and lots for summer homes. Popham paid George Saxon $500 down and promised an equal amount each month until the debt was paid. He attracted interest in Tallahassee, particularly among government officials. Notably, the Agricultural Commissioner bought a share, and was very aware of the shrimp and oyster industry in Apalachicola Bay.

Unfortunately for both companies, the economy entered a world-wide recession due to the 'Great War' already raging across Europe. Then the United States declared war on Germany in April, 1917 and joined Britain and France in World War I. Neither Popham nor the Lakeland company sold enough lots to repay Capital City Bank, and ownership reverted to George Saxon. Given the circumstances, the two men remained friends.

When his first venture in Apalachicola failed, William Popham refunded every subscriber's investment. Despite later claims made by U.S. government lawyers, there is no evidence that he intentionally cheated anyone.

Real estate sales in Tampa slumped in 1917. With Maude now pregnant, William Lee decided to get a job in a Jacksonville shipyard in support of his family and the war effort. The family moved to a houseboat on the St. Johns River after Willie got a job on a painting crew. He soon was made an inspector, but when the company heard that he was a writer, he was asked to take over as editor of its wartime newspaper, *The Hun Hammer*. His main aims were to sell war bonds to employees and maintain morale and productivity.

Just before their next visit to Apalachicola, the Pophams stopped in Tallahassee as they made their way across the state. Tallahassee had better hospitals than any town along the coast, and besides waiting for their baby to be born, William wanted to visit George Saxon to ask if the deed was settled so he could officially sell property on Saint George Island. On Christmas Eve, 1917, they were blessed with the birth of a son they named William Lee Popham, Jr.

When the war ended in 1918, Popham hit on a new idea. Instead of promoting individual ownership, he founded the Saint George Cooperative Colony, Unincorporated, with the idea of establishing a utopia in which all members of the colony would work building homes and share all income, which he promised would be $5 a day. He liked to refer to his investors as 'Comrades,' and may have known that the town of Eastpoint, across the bay from Apalachicola, had been founded on the progressive principle of sharing labor and profits.

Despite the name on the deed, Popham thought of the new organization as his 'Happiness Colony.' He mailed promotional brochures explaining how joyful life could be living on a Florida island with permanent income, and checks began to arrive. Anticipating visitors, Popham bought a boat called *The Governor* for express passage to the island, and began construction of an oyster packing plant at Nick's Hole to fulfill his promise of profit sharing.

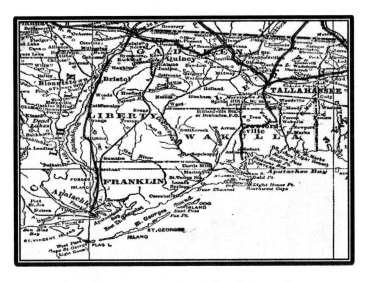

A map of Florida roads and railways from
1917 illustrates Popham's dilemma: With no
coastal highways and no bridges over the bay,
Saint George Island was hard to visit. To reach
Apalachicola, one had to drive south to Panacea
or take the railroad to Carrabelle and then take
a steamer. The alternative was to drive west of
Tallahassee and south along the river, or to take
the Apalachicola Northern Railway from Quincy
directly to Apalachicola.

The Bridge that Wasn't There

In early 1919, Willie laid a newspaper on James
Abbot's desk. "James, look at this advertisement in
the Tallahassee Democrat. It says wealthy Yankees
are taking the train to Thomasville, Georgia just to
spend the winter on a plantation. Why, they barely
have a catfish pond. What if those people knew
about Saint George Island and the Gulf of Mexico!"

"Yes, Thomasville bills itself as Rose City, and the civic association has planted flower gardens all around town," Abbott replied. "Thomasville became a winter destination after a railroad line was finished thirty years ago. There are mansions that are worth seeing if you ever visit up there."

"I am not so much concerned with Northerners, they are mostly heading to Miami. But people in Atlanta have never heard of Saint George Island, either, and we need to change that. Can you get the Board of Directors together by Thursday? Tell them we are taking *The Governor* to the island to have some photographs made, so call a photographer to take along," William replied.

"Of course, I'll have the secretary call them today. What exactly are you planning?"

"Maude and I are going to visit Atlanta in July, it is where we started our honeymoon. While we are there, I will tell newspaper reporters all the good news about the island and the Colony. We need some photographs to highlight the possibilities for people who have never been to the Gulf of Mexico."

By April, William Lee had received a manila envelope containing glossy photographs showing the Board of Directors riding the launch to the cove on Saint George Island. Other photos showed the businessmen looking over the surf or pointing at potential home sites for Colony members.

William, Maude and William, Jr., arrived in Atlanta and booked a suite in the Terminal Hotel. "I really like this hotel," Willie told the clerk at check-in, winking at Maude, "It is the most respectable one in Atlanta. By the way, do you know any good newspaper reporters?"

"Yes sir, you can call Ward Greene at the *Journal*. He has covered everything from sports to recruiting for the Great War. He also wrote a series on that Leo Frank murder trial. Mr. Greene knows how to tell a story."

"Ward Greene. Thank you, I will give him a call after we get settled."

The interview that Ward Greene thought might last 15 minutes turned into a four-hour marathon.

"We are founding a Happiness Colony on a beautiful island in the Gulf of Mexico, and people in Atlanta will be invited to join. Let me show you some photographs of Saint George Island and Apalachicola Bay," Willie began.

"What do you mean by 'Happiness Colony?'", Mr. Greene inquired.

"What could make a person happier than living at the beach in Florida sunshine and making five dollars a day all year? We are founding a City by the Sea on Saint George Island where every member shares in the profits of the whole enterprise. We have a seafood packing plant and are starting a sawmill, a livestock operation, a sugar refinery, a hotel, restaurant and movie theater!"

As they looked over the photographs, Ward Greene's curiosity was piqued. "Saint George Island, never heard of it. How did you find out about it?"

"James Abbott from Tampa told me about it. We work together in real estate. 'If you saw it, you would buy it,' he told me, and that is what I did. Bought it from George Saxon in Tallahassee and moved right down. I built a bungalow on the beach and have lived there for three years," Willie stated, beginning to 'stretch the truth' past normal limits.

"Then one day, it occurred to me that it was not right to own an island and not to share it. No sir, anyone who sees Saint George Island will love it just as much as I do. Now that the State has built a new steel bridge to the island, I want to open it up for anyone who wants to live in the best place in the world!"

"So now people can just drive over?", Mr. Greene asked.

"That's right, after the State built the new steel bridge for $220,000, they paved roads all along the middle of the island. It's a utopia with prime home sites ready to welcome the public! All the men will have steady work with time left over for fishing, hunting, and wooing their ladies to the sweet, sad song of the sea!"

Ward Greene's pictorial ran in the Sunday magazine of the Atlanta *Journal* on July 13, 1919. "There are few people who can out-elocute William Popham on the subjects of love, romance, and the splendor of beach living. But more than that, Mr. Popham has a clear vision of how Democracy can work. Members of the Happiness Colony will be free from strife, and have no need of police or jails. Besides oysters, fish, and lumber, children will be the main product of the happy colonists on Saint George Island!"

William brought copies of the Sunday supplement home and proudly showed them to James Abbott, with an extra copy for the editor of the Apalachicola *Times*. Abbott was flummoxed. "Willie, what is this about a bridge? Paved roads? A beach bungalow? You have taken this way too far, people will come and find out what is really here…and what is *not* here."

"James, I know there is no bridge. But there will be, and soon. I have dreamed every single thing I told Ward Greene, and my dreams are coming true!"

Abbott was upset and wrote to *The Journal*'s editor to correct the errors. "My associate means well, and believes that everything he says will come true. But the Board of Directors must stick to the facts, which are grand enough. *We must emphatically state that at present, there is no bridge to Saint George Island.*"

The Apalachicola *Times* ran an editorial noting that the new bridge was the safest in the country. "We have never had an automobile accident on our bridge. It has the best safety record of any in the United States!"

Ward Greene never joined The Happiness Colony and never tried to verify the existence of a bridge to Saint George Island. He bolstered his distinguished newspaper career by writing a series of novels. Years later, Walt Disney Productions used his short story about 'Happy Dan, the

Whistling Dog,' to create an animated feature called *Lady and the Tramp.*

Convinced that one day, a bridge would come, Willie Popham shrugged his shoulders and moved into the future. After an excellent start, Popham paid George Saxon $5000 towards the purchase. Abruptly, his plans were halted when a disgruntled employee who had been defeated in a bid to become secretary sued the Colony and forced it into receivership.

George Saxon once again wound up owning Saint George Island. Frustrated, Saxon began referring to Saint George Island as "My Albatross!"

Canned oysters were shipped from Apalachicola by railroad to destinations that were too far away to obtain fresh oysters in the shell. For closer cities, whole oysters were packed in rail cars with ice and sawdust.

The Oyster Growers' Cooperative Colony

Rather than giving up their quest for Saint George Island after relinquishing the deed a second time, the Popham family moved permanently to Apalachicola in 1920. One morning that year, Maude told Willie that she thought he had been on the right track with the Saint George Cooperative Colony.

"No one has been able to sell lots on Saint George Island solely for vacationing. You were right to offer to pay people a wage, that would give them a reason to stay rather than only to visit. The island is just too far even from Tallahassee. There must be some way to reach your goals," Maude observed.

"That is just what I have been thinking, Maude. Investors would want a way to live on the island and enjoy the beach and sea life while they earned an income. And the only answer I can come up with, besides selling real estate, is the oyster bottoms. By golly, I am heading to Tallahassee to talk with the Shell Fish Commissioner and learn more about the oyster business."

Willie obtained a copy of a survey of the oyster bottoms that the state had done in 1916 and a booklet on oyster culture published by the United States Bureau of Fisheries. He and his associates had assumed that landowners along the bay had the right to harvest oysters in adjoining waters, but the Shellfish Commissioner informed him that the state of Florida owned those rights, and was willing to lease them with an annual license fee.

"OK, we got off on the wrong foot last time," he told Maude. "But look at this report from the United States Bureau of Fisheries! It says that the average return for planting a bushel of shells is up to three bushels, sometimes as much as six bushels!"

"The Japanese have been cultivating oysters for hundreds of years. They use trees to build frames that oysters grow on. They seed the frames with spat, sink them in the bays and harvest the oysters, not to mention the pearls. Why, they are actually farming oysters! Can you beat that!"

Willie rapidly wrote some figures on ledger paper. "Maude, the oysters in Apalachicola Bay ought to be worth millions! If you farm oysters, harvests of 1,000 bushels per acre are possible, and you can get $3 a bushel with the quality of oyster we have. There are thousands of acres of oysters off Saint George Island!"

"Willie, I think you have hit on the right idea," Maude replied. We knew about land value, but had no notion of what the bay was worth. Why don't you explain this to James and the others and get started?"

On October 1, 1920, Maude and Willie together established the Oyster Growers' Cooperative Association. Maude served as treasurer, and Willie began promoting their new endeavor. He sent the following enthusiastic poem to the Apalachicola *Times*:

Apalachicola Is Good Enough For Me!

Like sea gulls, the oyster boats
Make this port their home-
And like the pelican that floats
O'er the rolling foam
This enterprising fleet
And boatmen worry-free,
Make Apalachicola good enough for me!

The Pophams began taking out full page advertisements extolling life on Saint George Island

and the joys of oystering in newspapers from Atlanta to St. Petersburg. For $250 paid in installments, subscribers could join the co-operative and live on the Gulf beach. For a higher price, they could buy several lots. When the oyster harvest began, all expenses would be paid by the oystering business.

Hopeful subscribers began sending checks, and Popham began advertising across the state and, indeed, across the country. So much mail poured in that the Post Office installed a large box to handle company mail. Popham often received 100 letters a day, with even more directed to the Co-Operative. He deposited the funds in the Apalachicola bank and opened an office on Water Street.

By late summer, Popham had raised $425,000. On December 10th, he paid George Saxon the full purchase price for Saint George Island. After almost five years of trying, William Lee Popham owned Saint George Island outright. George Saxon was free of his 'albatross,' and the Oyster King had been born. All he needed was a packing plant.

Men oystering from a sailboat, the usual method in Apalachicola Bay from 1880-1916. Except for the sails, the same methods are used today, though not many contemporaries wear vests while oystering. The man in the stern is culling harvested oysters

Oystering in Apalachicola Bay

In its normal condition the oyster is excellent food; and, if we assign it its rank among the shellfish, it will be, without dispute, the queen of the bivalves.

-Reverend Samuel Lockwood, 1874

Apalachicola Bay is the last place in the United States where oysters are harvested with oyster rakes by men in small boats. Elsewhere, dredges are used, or oysters are gathered by hand at low tide, or all oysters are produced by cultivation under sunken racks.

This is the only place where a visitor can observe men walking along the sideboards of 20-foot boats, vigorously working nine- to twelve-foot oyster rakes. Usually a second partner-sometimes a spouse- will be culling the pile of newly harvested shells, keeping only oysters at least 3 inches long. The rest are dumped back in the bay to continue growing. Presently, it is hard work to harvest 10 bags apiece, and the men get anywhere from $12 to $20 a bag. Many oystermen will fish for shrimp, crabs or grouper half of the year, or seek other kinds of seasonal work.

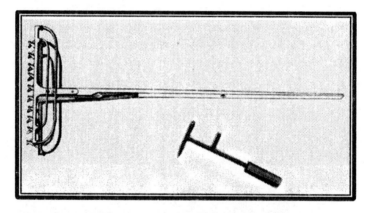

Custom-made oyster tongs, similar to the two-handled rakes that are still used in Apalachicola Bay to harvest oysters commercially and a culling iron with built-in measuring device for legal oysters. The tong handles, usually 9 to 12 feet long, open the rake by pivoting around the bolt in the middle. Tonging is the state-mandated harvesting method.

Oystermen do not tong oysters out of a desire to acquire wealth. They have chosen work in which they answer only to themselves and the packing houses where they sell their catch. Their reward is a rigorous life with days spent in an estuary of surpassing beauty. No two days on the water are the same, but each one brings its own glory, from soaring eagles to passing porpoises, with occasional whales and manatees—not to mention sharks and stinging jellyfish

As one life-long oysterman stated, "Once you get this water in your blood, working on this water, you know, nothing else satisfies you. Could you imagine being out here every day, and you get paid for it? This is paradise right here, it does not get any prettier than this bay."

Oyster shuckers' helper in about 1910 before child labor laws were enacted. Shuckers worked long hours for little pay. Photo by Lewis Hine, National Archive.

Act. IV. Gilding the Oyster

"Down by the sea lived a lonesome oyster,

Ev'ry day getting sadder and moister.

He found his home life awf'lly wet,

And longed to travel with the upper set."

-Cole Porter

The right to harvest and sell oysters from Apalachicola Bay was the key to the Oyster Growers' Cooperative. Popham's associates, including James Abbott, spun off a smaller company on the premise that if they bought land along the bay, they had the right to harvest oysters on adjoining bottom.

The smaller firm sued the state of Florida to acquire legal rights for the harvest. They argued that the 1804 Forbes Purchase of the Panhandle from Creek and Seminole Indians included fishing rights. The Florida Supreme Court disagreed and maintained that the state owned rights to the bottoms on the basis of the Riparian Act of 1856. With no way to link their land purchases to a sustainable harvest, the rival company folded, and its founders rejoined William Popham's firm.

Popham obtained a promise that he could lease rights to oyster bottoms from the State Agricultural Commissioner. Through his associate, "Island Man" William Roat, a lease for 500 acres was secured. Making a deal to purchase shells from the Acme Packing Plant in Apalachicola, William Popham hired men to begin planting oyster "cultch"

Crews harvesting oak trees for the Oyster Growers Cooperative. Wrapped with wire and sunk in the bay, the trees were used to cultivate seed oysters for the 'Popham Oyster Bottoms' next to Saint George Island.

to create a hard bottom for oyster spats to grow on. He purchased rights to the shellfish on bottoms adjacent to Little Saint George Island from the lighthouse keeper's family. Crews of hired men stabilized the shell beds with wire they ferried across from Apalachicola. They also harvested oak trees from Saint George Island, wired them together, and sunk the frames in the bay.

As checks continued to arrive, Popham bought land and oyster rights across the river mouth and west to 11 Mile oyster landing and the bottoms next to Saint Vincent's Island. Knowing the oyster harvest could begin in two years, he purchased two wharves in Apalachicola and a larger office on Market Street with 13 employees. Soon he would begin constructing a 61,000 square foot packing house.

Local newspapers began to refer to William Popham as 'The Oyster King," and he enjoyed the title. To accompany his poems and promotions about the joys of oystering, he had a map drawn up showing his lands and adjacent oyster bottoms.

Poet, Preacher, Promoter

In the1920's, most American workers were happy to earn a dollar a day. It is no surprise, then, that the following full page advertisement from William Popham caught their attention:

"Approaching the glad holiday season, we count our blessings with gratitude and look forward to Christmas. The writer is thankful for heaven's gift to his home of a golden-haired boy born three years ago on Christmas Eve, and also for being founder and president of the Oyster Growers Cooperative Association, *which will bless each of its 500 members with a lifetime income of two hundred dollars per month.*"

"We now quote from official document number 349 on Oysters and Methods of Oyster-Culture by the United States Government, that the usual average yield is "two or three times" the amount of the oysters planted. In other words, if we plant 100,000 barrels of oysters, we should harvest 200,000 barrels of oysters in the shell."

"At three gallons per barrel, the current price of $2 per gallon gives us an income of one million, two hundred thousand dollars per year ($1,200,000), to be divided equally among our 500 subscribers who own 50 preferred shares each. We will fully plant 100,000 barrels of shells in 1921, skip one year, and begin a full harvest in 1923. At that time, the dividends will begin to pour in."

"Any parent would do well to give each of his or her children a preferred share for their Christmas gift-for a lifetime cash income-to bless them each and every Christmas by this one gift of PERPETUAL blessing."

While the readers were assimilating this information, Popham the poet provided a lighter note on oyster farming:

Down in Florida on Our Oyster Farm

We live in Florida where the orange is king,
Where winter-time is just like spring.
When panics come, 'tis no alarm,
For we own a Florida oyster farm!
When the sun is warm, we'll sit in the shade
'Till harvest time and the crop is made;
Then we'll take our boat and ride
O'er the blue of the rolling tide;
It's just like play, 'mid Nature's charm
To harvest the crop of our oyster farm!

We'll cut no weeds and plow no rows;
No mules to feed, and need no hoes.
We'll hunt and fish while the oysters grow,
And linger where sea-breezes blow;
It beats the shop-it beats the store,
And every trip just calls for more.
We'll roll our bread in Florida honey,

103

And live like a king on "oyster money."

Take our advice, we mean no harm-
You'd better own a share in our oyster farm!

By "Florida honey," naturally Popham was referring to Tupelo honey from blossoming trees along the Apalachicola River. But what he loved was the fact that it rhymed with "oyster money."

Checks poured in and Popham kept on cooking up plans to invest the funds. Figuring he ought to get a percentage, he purchased the former Apalachicola home of renowned botanist, Alvan Chapman, and moved in with Maude and William Lee, Jr. Dr. Chapman had written *A Flora of the Southern United States* in 1860.

The Pophams began renovating the 1832 home to fit their style. The family added a garage with living quarters above it, and William purchased a gleaming red Willys-Knight automobile that was regarded as the classiest car in town.

Not stopping with automobiles, Popham purchased a speedboat powered by a 90 horsepower Curtiss airplane engine that was capable of making speedy trips across the bay and over to the train depot at Carrabelle. Willie decorated his conservative businessman's suit with a gold watch and chain, and started making plans to build oyster packing houses in Apalachicola and across from Saint Vincent Island.

Happiness—And Lots of It!

   Red Willys-Knight roadster acquired by
William Popham on his personal road to
happiness. No doubt he felt compelled to buy a
model advertised that it was "Willy's."

Little Sailors in the Bay

"I am almost sure to be attacked, before I have had time to squeeze my lemon, with inquiries why oysters are so dear, and why I do not do something to make them cheaper, as if I were Minister for Molluscan Affairs..."

-Thomas Henry Huxley, *Oysters and the Oyster Question,* 1883

Tasty animals that are sought out as food by humans, starfish, periwinkles, oyster drills and innumerable other enemies must become very good at reproduction. And so, however great the commotion on the docks and fish-houses of Apalachicola in 1923, the stirrings in the bay that spring were greater. Oysters that had reached their first year of life were maturing as males, whereas those that had been males the prior season were changing into females. To complicate matters, females that had just spawned were beginning to produce spermatozoa and change back into males for the rest of the season. Among oysters, spawning is as momentous as Easter, and no one wants to be left out of the parade.

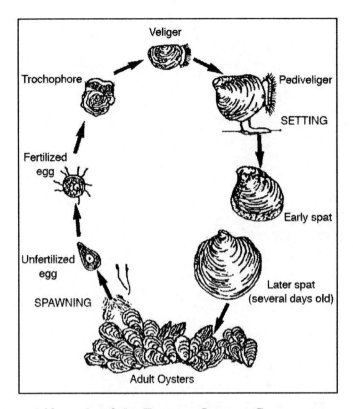

Life cycle of the Eastern Oyster, *Crassostrea virginica*. Fertilization and development as far as the veliger ("little sailor") take place in the female. After a few days floating free, the larva settles out on hard bottom and attaches. Although all of these stages may be called "spat," the term is best used for the newly attached oysters starting to grow on a hard surface.

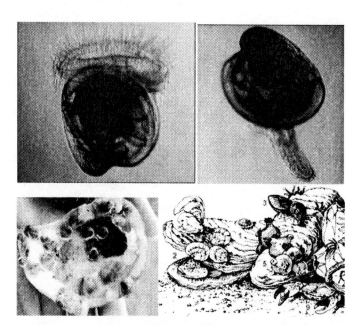

Highly magnified view of the free-floating veliger larva (top left) and the "sailor with a foot" or 'pedi-veliger' beginning to set (top right). Spat growing on a shell are shown (bottom left) and a portion of an oyster bar with spat and mature oysters is at lower right.

Oysters are sequential hermaphrodites, and it seems that most of the younger, smaller animals are male, whereas the larger, older ones start the season as females. After all, it takes a great deal of energy to produce two million egg cells in season, and probably much less to produce spermatozoa. Exchanging gametes is not easy because the two sexes are tightly fastened to whatever substrate they landed on at the end of their larval stage. Oysters cannot "hook up," so they follow different rules.

Beginning in April, millions of sex cells in the female begin to enlarge, fill with substances that will nourish the eggs after fertilization, and loosen from the ovary. As the eggs free themselves, a water current produced by thousands of lashing cilia moves the eggs to a location under the gills and shell-forming mantle. The water current also draws in spermatozoa from neighboring males, and the tiny white egg cells become fertilized and develop a dark spot. The dark spots grow to become free-swimming larvae called veligers. Most eggs mature together, and the females open and close their shells with enough force to expel clouds of young into surrounding waters.

Veligers are little sailors that float free on tidal currents for a few days, and may be carried miles from their native spawning beds. Gradually, a foot forms, and the larvae stop swimming and settle to the seabed. If the bed is soft, the larvae have no chance of growing, but if the bed is rock, shell, gravel or wood, the oysters settle on the surface and attach themselves firmly by secreting shell material from the lip of their mantles.

In the spring of 1922, William Popham had hired crews of men to cut oak trees on Saint George Island, bind the trees together with wire mesh, and sink them in the bay to provide places for young oysters to attach. He had read about this method in accounts of European and Japanese oyster culture. There is no record that any other company in Apalachicola had tried this, and it proved to be successful.

Popham also hired watermen to haul barges laden with piles of oyster shells into the bay and dump them in areas that had soft bottom. In some areas, oystermen move spawning oysters into shallow waters or ponds where they can favor the production of seed oysters on hard bottom. The seed oysters are then harvested and taken to areas with hard bottom where they can mature. By the end of the first year in Apalachicola Bay, their average size is close to three inches and they are growing rapidly. Although some could be harvested, it is preferable to wait until the second summer, when most will be 3-5 inches long and most can be kept.

**Promotional map drafted by William Popham
to depict his land purchases and the oyster bars
he had leased from the State of Florida by 1922.**

Romance by the Sea

William Lee gathered his associates in his offices on Market Street early in 1922 and outlined his master plan. "We now own Saint George Island outright, and I have purchased rights to 500 acres of oyster bottom from Nick's Hole over to West Pass. To succeed for our investors, we need to start producing income as soon as we can do it."

"So, this year, we need to continue planting seed oysters in the bay, but we also need land along the bay wherever there are oyster bars offshore. I propose buying any available land from Apalachicola west to Indian Pass so we have access to the oyster bars off Saint Vincent Island."

"We will also need wharves in Apalachicola where we can build an oyster packing plant. Mr. Roat, I want you to tour modern plants in the Northeast with me and find out which manufacturers we need to contact. I want three plants. We have one on the island, we need one in Apalachicola and another can be built at 11 Mile west of town if we can get the land."

"So this year, we are going to be buying land, leasing oyster bottoms, planting natural oyster beds, creating new beds, building factories, and selling lots on Saint George. We can continue harvesting oysters for some of our income, but the key, the real key here, is to use the oysters and maybe shrimp to generate permanent income for investors who buy our lots."

"Now here's the big new push. I am going to announce a Million Dollar Bond Plan. Current investors can transfer into it, and new investors can be recruited. We need 4,000 investors at $250 each, a down payment of $25 and $5 a month until they pay the full subscription."

"This is a business, of course, but I have a dream. I want to be able to share Saint George Island with our investors. It is too perfect a place to keep to ourselves. Gentlemen, that is the future as I see it!"

William's father, Virgil, died in 1922 and his mother, Clara, came to live with William, Maude, and William, Jr., in the Chapman House. The family also included "Silent Jim" Estes, Maude's eccentric but harmless brother.

When not doing yard work, Jim walked the streets of Apalachicola, tamping tobacco into his pipe and talking to himself. If a passer-by stopped to ask why he kept talking to himself, Jim would answer, "Because I enjoy conversation with intelligent people!"

By 1923, Popham's enterprises had purchased wharves in Apalachicola and the 11-Mile oyster landing opposite Saint Vincent Island. The firm purchased over 20,000 acres along the bay and 40,000 acres inland. Popham started a new venture, selling real estate for a 5% commission, and opened a branch office in Tallahassee to cultivate interest among residents and government officials. A large salt water aquarium with oysters growing in it claimed the attention of anyone who entered the lobby.

Popham rented eight rooms of office space on Market Street to accommodate staff for his businesses. He acquired a 2,000 year-old, giant oyster shell from Australia and hung it like a gong in the sales room. Clients would ring it like a bell, having no idea that it had not been harvested from Apalachicola Bay.

Dormant for a hundred years, Apalachicola suddenly came to life, with visitors arriving daily to visit Saint George Island and do business with the Oyster Growers Cooperative. Popham drafted a map displaying the company's holdings, prominently depicting "Popham Lands" and "Popham Oyster Bottoms," and hired a motor launch to take visitors to Saint George Island where they could inspect the holdings.

To cap the activities of 1923, Popham began construction of a two-story oyster packing plant, and filled its 61,000 square feet with the most modern equipment available. The insides were enameled in white and brightly lit so it could operate at night. Outside, oyster shells spelled out POPHAM OYSTER FACTORY NO. 1.

William Lee's enthusiasm brought all his talents to fruition. His poetry and prose lauded the oyster industry and beach living in Florida. Churches invited him to give sermons, and his oratorical gifts flourished. When he spoke, people ferried across Apalachicola Bay from Eastpoint and Carrabelle to hear him. Crowds overflowed the churches, just as they formerly filled big tents on the Chautauqua circuit.

Popham Oyster Factory No. 1 in 1923 (top) and in 2013 (bottom). Covered docks at right were used to unload oyster boats. The building is next to the bridge at the Maritime Museum.

Calvary Baptist Church offered William a chance to become its minister, but in the heyday of his oyster operations, Popham declined the request. Earlier in his life, this would have presented a major conflict, but William Lee no doubt was directing his prayers toward success for his oyster and real estate ventures. Much as he loved to share the Gospel, his desire to share Saint George Island was greater.

For once, Popham's timing was fortunate even concerning the weather. No hurricanes hit Apalachicola Bay between 1915 and 1925.

Although a drought cycle began in the 1920's, it did not become severe until the 1930's when the dust bowl began. With few tropical storms and adequate rainfall, oysters thrived in Apalachicola Bay and harvests were excellent. Even Nature was providing good reasons for Popham to be optimistic.

The Apalachicola *Times* observed, "He has done more for his investors than he told them he would do. William Lee Popham is an unusual promoter, who is very different from promoters who have little or no regard for their promises."

Esteem for William Popham peaked in 1923. He was nominated for mayor and accepted, but did little campaigning. The townspeople were very aware that Popham wanted to increase business in Franklin County. In one earlier speech, he had stated,

> "I love every acre of her sunny soil; I love every drop of sparking water in the great Gulf that kisses her border…I love every business-man here, and want him to prosper in his business…I love every man, woman and child in Franklin County, for whom there is not one that I would not rise from my bed at midnight and walk miles in darkness to favor, or aid in time of need."

He was elected Mayor of Apalachicola in November, 1923, with only two opposing votes, and held the office for two years.

Numerous potential investors visited Apalachicola and spent money at its hotels and restaurants, and most businesses thrived. William Popham felt that his prospects were sublime, and penned a poem to the bivalve that had made it possible:

"The Oyster Harvest Moon"

Beneath the oyster harvest moon
Serene from all alarm
Where harvest time is coming soon
Is our Florida oyster farm;
And with a hundred thousand barrels-
Where winter rivals June-
Our planted oysters thrive and grow
Beneath the harvest moon.

Left out of the new prosperity, however, were the rival seafood packing plants, whose owners were now vying with the Oyster Growers Cooperative for limited harvesting grounds. Jealousy was inevitable, and did not take long to show its jade-green head.

Adult willet shorebird with three young in Saint George Island State Park—Huey, Dewey and Louie?

A 'Spat' with Rivals

"Mr. Popham, a gentleman from town wishes to speak to you in private," William's receptionist said as he entered the office one Monday morning. As he turned, William saw a stocky, muscular man with weathered features getting up from a chair. The man was dressed in denim overalls, tall boots and a red plaid work shirt. Recognizing Carl Carver from church, William smiled broadly and extended his hand, "Carl, it's good to see you! How are you this morning and what's on your mind?" As they shook hands, he noted Carl's callused hands and powerful grip.

"We'd better go in your office, Mr. Popham," Carl replied. Once inside, he closed the door and continued, "I grew up right here and started oystering when I was twelve. Helped Dad with the boat before that, he would catch and I would cull.

Thing is, oystering is hard work. You need to be on the water before sun-up, and you need to work whether it's fair weather or blowing up twenty knots. You work in the cold and you work in the heat. If storms get too bad, you don't work at all. People do it because they want to work on the bay, but they sure don't do it to make a pile of money. So let me guess, you have never actually oystered yourself, have you?"

Still smiling, William admitted that he had not. "I prefer to hire men who know the business, and consider it a good thing to be able to offer steady work."

Carl nodded but William could see that the man's jaw was clenched. "There is not much money in tonging oysters. Back in 1912, I went into business, figuring if I had a packing plant, I could manage the business and not have to be on the water every day for a wage. You know my business, West Point Packing Company." William nodded.

"Now you come in here and claim you have leased all the oyster bottoms." Carl's voice was quiet but angry. "My crews tell me that your men run them off from places they have oystered for twenty years. Let me tell you, sir, I am not going to stand by and let an outsider rob me of my livelihood."

Popham's face flushed, and he stopped smiling. "Now wait a minute, Carl, I have never done anything except praise Apalachicola and try to develop oystering. You know that."

"That may be what you think, it's not how I see it. I can't pay my men five dollars a day like you claim. You and Henry Ford. Some of my best crews have gone to work for you, and my income is down about half just this year. Well, I won't stand for it. I have read your brochures, and am aware that you could not pay your investors what you claim if you harvested every last oyster in Florida. You, sir, are a fraud, and I intend to report you as such!" He turned and started out the door.

"Wait, Carl, there is enough resource for all of us out there! My crews are planting 100,000 barrels of shells every year and seeding them with oyster spat. It's God's bounty and we can share the harvest."

"God's bounty? You seem to think that every word you speak is true even when the facts are against you. I shall make sure the Shell Fish Commissioner knows what you are up to. The Devil take you, Popham!" Carl walked out without turning to look back or close the door. Of the hundreds of people William had met in Franklin County, Carl Carver was the first man to object openly to his operations.

Two weeks later, a vessel named *Seafoam* pulled up to Popham Oyster Factory No. 1, displaying the great seal of Florida on its bow. A tall, uniformed man stepped onto the docks and asked to speak to the plant supervisor. It was T.R. Hodges, the Florida Shell Fish Commissioner.

By the end of the day, Mr. Hodges had checked the licenses of every oyster crew, inspected the shucking and packing operation, and made it clear that he objected to seeding oysters at a depth greater than could be reached with tongs.

"Mr. Popham, I noticed two dredge boats next to your docks. It seems to me that you plan to harvest oysters by illegal means," he stated.

"People are complaining about your methods, and I intend to see to it that you follow the letter of the law with no exceptions. My office can and will shut down your operation if we find you dredging oysters on state leases. And I have learned from the Agricultural Commissioner that your firm has purchased 90% of all state leases in Apalachicola Bay."

William protested that his methods of oyster cultivation were described in a United States Government publication, and that Hodges was wrong about his harvesting methods. "We will never harvest any State oyster bars by any method except raking," he said. "It is my understanding that private holdings may be harvested by other means, and we will defend our procedures in court if need be."

"Well, my friend, that might become necessary. You had better watch your steps. Are you really willing to take on the State of Florida?" Hodges departed, leaving a chill in the room.

Popham tried to joke his way out from under his gloomy feelings. "Oh, well," he mused, "This is the oyster business. I suppose there is no way to avoid a 'spat' or two." The feeble humor did not improve his forebodings.

Modern shrimp boat with nets up traveling down the Apalachicola River mouth to the bay.

The Dignitaries

Four months after he took office as Mayor of Apalachicola, Popham received a telephone call from William Jennings Bryan. "I am visiting every county seat in northern Florida to raise money for the university and campaign to be elected delegate to the Democratic presidential convention. Would it be possible to arrange a visit the week of May 15th? I will need to make a speech in a suitable venue that could accommodate several hundred people."

"Yes, please plan on staying at my home while you are here. If you take the train from Tallahassee, I can send a private boat to ferry you over from Carrabelle." Mayor Popham asked his secretary to reserve the Dixie Theater and announced that a parade would be held and automobile traffic would be restricted.

Willie asked Maude if she would prepare a seafood dinner with fresh oysters and speckled trout to highlight Apalachicola's reputation for quality seafood. On the day the train arrived, Popham hired a boat captain to drive his motorboat, the *Lady Popham*, to Carrabelle. They landed at the steamboat dock and walked to the train depot just before the express was due. They waited with a photographer from the Apalachicola Times, and had no trouble picking out the Bryan party.

William Jennings Bryan stared at Willie for a moment. "Excuse me, but have we ever met? You look familiar, especially your eyes."

Willie shook Bryan's hand and nodded, "Oh yes, some years back, Clyde Buckley asked me to introduce you to the Chautauqua Association in Louisville."

"Oh, yes, now I remember! You are the preacher Clyde told me about. What are you doing here in Florida?"

"I will show you, we have plenty of time." As they motored back across the bay, Willie pointed to Saint George Island. "That is the gem of Apalachicola Bay," he commented. "To develop the island is the focus of my life, in fact, my calling. I had to turn down being minister for that 'siren.'"

"Looks good to me," replied Bryan over the roar of the Curtiss engine, "But if you want to see real development, you ought to come to Miami. The Venetian Pool is the largest in the world, and the Biltmore Hotel dwarfs anything I saw coming through Tallahassee."

Back in Apalachicola, Willie had parked his Willys-Knight at the marina. The two men moved the luggage to the boot of the car and Willie drove

Bryan to his home to meet Maude and relax before showing him the town.

"I find it interesting that we both moved to Florida," Willie noted. "Maude and I began in Tampa. What influenced you?"

"Nebraska winters are hard on an old man," Bryan replied. "After Henry Flagler built the Florida East Coast Railway with a direct connection to New York, we built a winter home in Coconut Grove that we like to call *Villa Serena*. It is a great place to relax after a speaking tour. A couple of years ago, a man named George Merrick decided to build the Miami suburb of Coral Gables, and hired me to speak to interested parties. He invites crowds of them down on the train and my job is to sell them on life in Florida."

"Amazing," replied Willie, "I was also drawn into Florida real estate. In fact, your speech in Louisville helped convince me that farming or preaching was not to be my career. That island we passed on the way back from Carrabelle became my destiny. My associates and I are developing Saint George Island in a package that includes a seafood plant to generate income for our investors. Around here, the newspapers call me 'The Oyster King.' Who could have guessed where two farm boys like us would wind up?"

Warren G. Harding, US President-elect, selects a golf club from his caddy, Rosie the elephant. Carl Fisher used the elephant to welcome prospective investors to his Miami Beach real estate venture.

Bryan nodded in agreement. "Over on the East Coast, there are few oysters as far as I know. George built the Venetian, a giant swimming pool, a golf course, and Biltmore put in the most beautiful hotel you have ever seen. All it takes to sell people on Coral Gables is Florida sun and sports when New York is freezing up. A man named Carl Fisher built the Lincoln Highway across the country and followed up with the Dixie Highway to Miami. He named the ocean shore Miami Beach and bought an elephant to greet visitors. Fisher is the one who put up the sign in Times Square that says, 'It's always June in Miami!'"

Willie nodded, "There is no land boom here, but Maude and I have been promoting Saint George Island too. Our dilemma is having no direct access by land except a small railroad spur. It sounds as if you folks on the East Coast are on a whole different scale."

"You are right there. Rumors have it that Merrick and Fisher are worth over a hundred million each. George pays me an obscene amount to make speeches so his 'binder boys' can sell lots to the tourists. I am not getting more involved than that, I am putting my energy into the next platform for the Democratic Party. I never thought success was about money, it is a matter of values."

Before Willie could do more than nod, Maude called the men to supper. As host, Willie said grace, and then Maude served pecan-coated speckled trout and baked oysters. "Delicious, the best I have ever had," Bryan commented, "I do appreciate your friendship and hospitality."

In the morning, Willie drove Mr. Bryan along the waterfront and showed him the ice works, the electric and telephone company, and Popham Oyster Factory No. 1. At noon, they led a parade along Water Street up to the Dixie Theater for Mr. Bryan's appeal. After the speech, the dignitary said good-bye to the Pophams and returned to Carrabelle to catch the next train to Tallahassee.

William Jennings Bryan was elected as a Florida delegate to the national Democratic Convention for 1924 but was not able to raise sufficient funds to start a Young Men's Christian Association building on the University of Florida campus. He visited William and Maude Popham twice during the 1920's.

Henry Flagler's Florida East Coast Railway opened the route from New York City to Miami and Key West. Along with Carl Fisher's Dixie Highway, the transportation routes led to the Florida Land Boom of the 1920's that collapsed in 1925.

Things Fall Apart

> Turning and turning in the widening gyre
> The falcon cannot hear the falconer;
> Things fall apart; the centre cannot hold...
> The best lack all conviction, while the worst
> Are full of passionate intensity.

--William Butler Yeats

By the summer of 1923, the Oyster Growers Cooperative Association and lot sales on Saint George Island were both thriving. The new packing house was running, and shipments of oysters were being sent to buyers by railroad. The company had real income, albeit not the millions Willie had foreseen. Nevertheless, subscribers were arriving to view their lots on Saint George Island and investigate prospects for building cottages there. After years of struggling, William's plan—or scheme, to some detractors—was working perfectly, and he had become wealthy by Gulf Coast standards.

William had served as President of the Chamber of Commerce and was presently Mayor of Apalachicola. He gave occasional sermons at Calvary Baptist church and published poems and anecdotes in the Apalachicola *Times*. He enjoyed planning excursions to Saint George Island and inviting friends and business leaders along.

William and Maude had made far more friends than enemies in Franklin County. With business booming, it is doubtful that they were prepared for the double dose of trouble that began in the summer of 1922.

The Co-Operative Colony's founding papers stated, "We shall have no organization, and by having no organization, will save red-tape reports to state departments, corporation taxes, corporation income taxes, fat fees to politicians...and personal liabilities." It took the Bureau of Internal Revenue of the U.S. Treasury Department two years to notice this lapse. In 1922, agents filed a $200,000 tax lien against William and Maude for three years of unpaid income taxes.

The United States had only begun imposing income taxes in 1914 after the 16th amendment was ratified. During World War I, the rate for incomes over $100,000 was increased to 64%, and was still 56% in 1922. The Bureau had no access to company records, but must have assumed that Popham was earning close to $100,000 a year during that period.

The government placed all properties owned by the Oyster Growers Co-Operative Association under attachment until the taxes were paid—but after the second dire event took place, the taxes never would be paid.

In October, 1923, William Popham was summoned to Washington, D.C., to testify at a hearing concerning his possible fraudulent use of the U.S. mail. The Post Office contended that Popham had used funds received through his mailings for personal gain. He returned to Apalachicola, but received word in December that the government had terminated his use of the U.S. mail due to apparent fraud. A jury trial would be scheduled in the Fifth District Federal Court to determine guilt.

Unable to use the U.S. mail, William Popham's real estate ventures imploded. Even if he placed advertisements in newspapers, any letters addressed to him would be confiscated. The flow of checks dried up.

Popham blamed his rivals, and particularly Shell Fish Commissioner Hodges, for stirring up the trouble. He characterized his rivals as "those who by envy, malice and hatred, are trying to ruin a great and legitimate development of Florida's natural resources of sea foods, and opening up of the Gulf territory."

Most residents supported Popham's claims. A petition to oust Commissioner Hodges was signed by one thousand Franklin County residents, mostly involved with the seafood industry. Given that roughly 4,000 people lived in Apalachicola, that is an astonishing level of support. The Tallahassee Dispatch sent a reporter to interview residents, and an article was published stating "that Popham's development work should be retarded by such men as our Shell Fish Commissioner is more than we can understand."

Despite the protest, the reviled Hodges was not removed from his state position, and the petition had no impact on the federal indictment. The trial was slated for January, 1924 but was delayed. Popham's defense team argued that the district was too small to have had two grand juries empanelled at once, and moved to quash the trial. However, the government lawyers requested a delay so they could prepare fresh arguments. The judge stunned the defense team by granting the continuance, even though he dismissed all charges except mail fraud.

Although William Popham thought he would win the legal case, he decided that his troubles should not be allowed to disrupt his company's operations. He and Maude resigned as trustees of the company, and a judge appointed two new trustees of what became known as the Popham Trust Estate. In 1925, the district court at Pensacola ruled that the Estate, and not the Bureau of Internal Revenue, had claim to the company's properties. For a time at least, the Oyster Growers Co-Operative could continue to operate, and sales on Saint George Island could go on.

Control of the company passed to trustee Edward Porter in 1926. An offer of $625,000 to purchase the company, including its holdings on Saint George Island, was made in 1926. During an ensuing legal battle, Popham transferred the deed to Saint George Island to his mother, and Porter purchased the remaining estate for $300,000.

Needing to make a living, Popham started a new enterprise called Florida Wholesale Land Company, and advertised that "The Best Investment on Earth, Is the Earth Itself." The Post Office relented and allowed his new company to send and receive mail. Unfortunately, a new indictment was handed down on September 8th, with trial slated for early 1925. Popham's defense team managed to change the venue from Pensacola to Tallahassee.

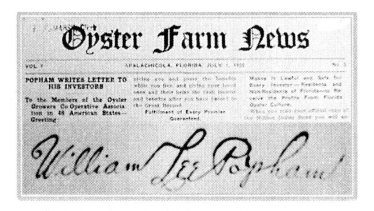

Copy of *Oyster Farm News* from 1922 in which William Popham announced his Million Dollar Bond Plan and invited his investors to increase their subscriptions. Bottom shows his stamped signature. Both items are from the transcript of his trial in the Fifth Circuit Court in 1925.

The Trial

When the Popham trial began, the audience overflowed the courtroom. The Tallahassee crowd was especially eager to hear Popham's oratorical defense against unjustified accusations.

Expecting quick action, the crowd was disappointed as government lawyers read page after page of details concerning seven charges into the record. The defendants had used the United States mail service to solicit investments that falsely promised lifetime income. There were to be oyster factories, button factories, brick and concrete factories, and amusement parks. The oyster harvest alone would produce income greater than any worker in Apalachicola had ever attained. Investors were swindled and received no dividends of any kind. Government charges would be proved by calling upon testimony from 92 witnesses.

James Armstrong of Montgomery, Alabama was called to the stand. "I came over with a group of investors in 1921 and inspected the properties. I decided Mr. Popham was as good as his word, and invested $900."

"Sir, what happened to change your mind?"

"Mr. Popham started soliciting for an enlarged plan. He called it his Million Dollar Bond Plan, and told us the bond would ensure that no investor ever lost a cent. I did not want to send more money, and requested a refund."

"And did you ever receive your money back?"

"No sir, not a cent. Mr. Popham wrote and asked me to come talk to him. He said that he would satisfy me that the investment was sound and would refund my money if he could not do it."

"But he never did refund your money, did he?"

"No sir, I got nothing back."

Next, the defense attorneys cross-examined Mr. Armstrong. "Sir, did you receive a certificate proving your ownership of five lots on Saint George Island?"

"Well, yes, and I still have those certificates."

"Sir, those lots are valued at $1000 each. It seems that you have a substantial return on your investment."

"Except that I have not been able to get any of it back. Mr. Popham said we would be making $200 a month by now, so where is it?"

"The U.S. Bureau of Taxes has put a lien on the company's bank accounts. The government itself is to blame for this situation, and in fact is hounding a totally honest concern. The defense yields."

Undeterred, the prosecution called on Mrs. Rose Shannon of Tallahassee.

"I sent Mr. Popham $200 in 1921, and got one of his certificates in the mail," she stated. ""Then in March of 1922, a letter came requesting more money for his Bond Plan. I did not want to go in on it and asked for my money back."

"And did he satisfy your request?"

"No sir. All I got was more letters about how well all his punk companies were doing and a copy of the Oyster Farm News with more poems. He asked me to come see him but I never got any part of it back, not one plugged nickel."

The defense attorneys asked if she knew that the government had seized the company's bank accounts?

"Yes, I heard that. But you would think they could come up with $200. I was not in it for that island property, I needed a dividend."

"Ma'am, you said you have a certificate of ownership. Did you ever visit Saint George Island?"

"Yes, my husband and I went out there on the boardwalk and over to the hotel. By the time we got back to the boat, I had chased a rattlesnake off the boardwalk, stepped in the sand spurs, and the gnats had chewed up my ankles. They itched like fire for two days!"

Two men on the jury laughed out loud along with most of the audience, and the judge rapped his gavel. "Order, order in the court!" Embarrassed, the defense attorney yielded the floor.

Head in his hands, Willie stared at the table in front of him. "You must let me testify," He requested, "I am the only one here who knows the truth."

"Impossible. That would open a can of worms, and there would be no way to put a lid on it. Do you want them to call Maude to testify against you?"

349

OYSTERS

AND

METHODS OF OYSTER-CULTURE,

WITH

NOTES ON CLAM-CULTURE.

BY

H. F. MOORE,
Assistant, United States Fish Commission.

Title page of the U.S. Bureau of Fisheries publication number 349 on oyster culture that inspired William Popham to conceive of a plan for residents of Saint George Island to secure a permanent income from oyster farming. Shell Fish Commissioner Hodges maintained that the methods and yields were unrealistic for Florida waters.

The Oystermen Speak

The prosecution called C.L. Sheppard to the stand. "Sir, please tell us how you know the defendants."

"I run the Acme Packing Plant in Apalachicola; we specialize in fresh and canned oysters. Mr.

Popham approached me in 1920 to ask about buying shell from us."

"So you are very familiar with the oyster industry. Can you tell the court how much income your business can generate per year?"

"Certainly. Top quality fresh oysters sell for $2.50 a barrel. Lower grade ones that we can go for $1.75."

"And how many oysters are harvested each year?"

"The bay produces around 150,000 barrels a year. So you are talking about maybe $300,000 a year from oysters, tops."

All right, suppose Mr. Popham's company got all of that and distributed it equally to 1,000 investors, how much would they be getting?"

"That would be about $300 each, but it will never happen!"

"Why do you say that?"

"There are 15 packing plants in Apalachicola and I was talking about the total from all of them. Oysters are about a third of the income, because most houses also pack shrimp and fin fish. In a good year, the total income from Apalachicola Bay might be a million dollars."

"So, would you consider Mr. Popham's claims to be fraudulent?"

"Sir, William Popham is my friend, and I never considered anything he said to be false. He always paid me what he said he would in any of our dealings. But yes, it would be stretch to earn even $100 a month from oystering for all those investors."

The defense attorney tried to rebut the claim of fraud in cross-examination. "Mr. Sheppard, do the men who work for you practice oyster cultivation? Do they plant barrels of seed oysters on the bars?"

"Not generally. Most of my men harvest from the natural bars. We sell most of our shell to the railroad to use for fill when they lay tracks."

"Are you aware of the official government statements that planting oyster beds with shell can return two barrels of harvested oysters for each barrel of seed?"

"I have heard Mr. Popham say that. But in my experience, you are doing pretty well to get 200 barrels per acre even when you plant 500. If you plant more than that, all you are doing is covering up the bed. It does not pay. We never planted more than 200 barrels an acre when we tried it."

"Very well, but how much shell did you sell to Mr. Popham's Co-operative?"

"Easily 100,000 barrels a year, sometimes more. He was trying to expand the natural beds around his 500 acre lease."

"Would you say that the Co-operative could get a return of 100,000 barrels based on that kind of planting?"

"Under the best circumstances. Trouble is, some of that land off Little Saint George is not hard bottom. You would find it hard to get 100 barrels an acre in a good year. I would guess that the total would be less than 50,000 barrels a year."

Frustrated, the defense yielded and the prosecution called Florida Shell Fish Commissioner Hodges to testify.

"Commissioner Hodges, how would you evaluate the claims that were advertised through the U.S. mail service by William Popham?"

"He said that the income would be $100 to $200 a month. Mr. Popham would need to harvest 48 million bushels of oysters to pay his investors one hundred dollars a month. That amount would be three times more than the entire annual Florida harvest."

The prosecutor continued, "The following poem was included in advertisements that were sent out in the U.S. mail. I would like to read it into the record and ask for your opinion."

The Land Where the Oyster Grows

By William Lee Popham

O, give me the land where the oyster grows
Where the sea and the river meet-
Where water never overflows
And the air is fresh and sweet;
Where sunsets leave an afterglow
O'er fields of liquid gold-
O, give me the land where the oysters grow-
Where the young cannot grow old.

139

Goodbye to the fields of Dad's old farm,
Goodbye to the plow and hoe;
'Hard work' to me has lost its charm
Where the weeds and grasses grow;
I'll plant my oysters in the deep-
Where nature makes 'em grow
Into harvest while I sleep
While sea tides come and go.

O, give me the land that the rainbow spans
And points to a pot of gold;
And here I'll fill my pots and pans
Where a million waves have rolled.
I've found the land where the rainbow ends
Of which Irish fairies told-
Where the oysters have become my friends,
And THEY'RE my pots of gold.

Everyone in the courtroom except for the defense
team and Commissioner Hodges grinned as the
poem was read. James Abbott grimaced and
averted his eyes.

"What is your opinion, Commissioner Hodges?"

"I have met most of the men in the oyster trade
in Florida. Most of them would be amused by the
poem, but none of them ever found a pot of gold on
an oyster bed! Claiming that 4,000 investors could
earn $100 a month from Apalachicola Bay is folly."

"But sir, is that folly tantamount to fraud?"

"Given what I know, I would consider it fraud.
What is very clear from the poem is that Mr.
Popham has never tonged oysters. They may grow

while you sleep, but you have to be awake and on the docks by 5 A.M. to start the harvest."

With the statements from the oystermen and Commissioner Hodges, the accusation of fraud seemed mathematically incontrovertible. For reasons that have never been clear, the defense attorneys did not rebut the arguments, and never allowed William Popham to testify, despite knowing that the entire courtroom audience wanted him to speak.

The judge repeated the charges and instructed the jury concerning the weight of the evidence and possible outcomes.

After two days of deliberation, the Tallahassee jury found William Lee Popham guilty of mail fraud, and the judge sentenced him to four years of confinement in the federal penitentiary in Atlanta.

Maude, Clara and William, Jr., were distraught at the trial's outcome, but William seemed outwardly unperturbed. "I consider the verdict to be the Lord's judgment," he said. "I do not know what I have done wrong, but I must accept the result, bow my head, and pray for guidance. The Lord is offering me a chance for redemption."

William had secretly feared a negative outcome. Earlier that year, he had transferred title to Saint George Island from his and Maude's names to his mother, Clara. As 1926 began, Clara Popham was legally the sole owner of Saint George Island, and the government could not take possession of the island.

Unlike her son, Clara was not interested in selling Gulf beach property.

Raking and culling oysters from a sailboat about 1909.   Lewis Hine photo, National Archives.

Consequences

"William, I have considered you to be my closest friend for 12 years," James Abbott agonized one morning after the verdict. "You know I never have objected to your way of promoting our business as long as you stuck to the facts. But what I see now is that the government made its case, you really did do what they accused, and the jury believed them, too."

"James, I have always felt the same way about you. You are my best friend, the one who introduced me to Apalachicola and this wonderful bay. Don't worry about the verdict for a moment; I am sure it can be overturned when we get an appeal."

"You don't see it yet, do you, William?" Abbott replied. "The company never got around to sending dividends to our investors. You really did use their money to buy your house, a new car, and that boat you use for show during the Fourth of July boat races."

"James, I am sorry to hear you talking like that. We founded the company; no one expected we would operate it for free. Keep in mind, the island has appreciated in value by twenty-fold since we bought it."

"William, there is an element of truth in most things you say, but then you stretch it. You did not just buy a house, you bought a mansion. Everything you bought had to be the biggest and best in town, the finest car, the most sumptuous clothing, the fastest boat. It was not necessary, and you used investors' money to do it. Now the law caught on. You are telling yourself it is God's will, but that is not it. You broke the law and dragged us all into the financial mess."

"I was going to tell you that despite the verdict, I remain the happiest man in Florida," William replied. "But not if I lose your friendship."

"It saddens me to have to disagree with you," James replied. "But you do know why your lawyers wouldn't let you speak at the trial, don't you? It was that newspaper article about that damnable bridge that never existed. All the prosecutors had to do was list every falsehood in the article, and you would have had to admit to lying."

William folded his hands and stared at the floor with bowed head as a tear trickled down his face. "James, James, you know I had to express what was in my heart and in my dreams. If I am guilty of anything, it is wanting to share my dreams."

James shook his head as he left. "The case seems solid to me, I think you better prepare for the worst. The government is using you as an example of every fraudulent land scheme in Florida, which is saying something." He turned away and walked out of the office.

The verdict was appealed to the Fifth Circuit Court, but the original verdict was upheld. As 1926 began, William Lee Popham began settling his affairs while his defense team appealed the verdict to the Court of the Last Resort.

Two Years in the Atlanta Federal Penitentiary

The verdict of mail fraud was appealed to the United States Supreme Court. Popham felt that if he were innocent, the Lord would see to it that a new trial was held. If the verdict was upheld, he assumed the judgment was just. In November, he learned that the Supreme Court had refused to review the conviction.

A summons was issued requesting that William Popham meet the United States Marshalls in Tallahassee in November, 1926. When Popham met the Tallahassee train to the Atlanta prison, he was carrying a heavy suitcase. The U.S. Marshall asked him why he needed so much, given his destination.

"Oh, there are no clothes here, just writing paper and all my books. I plan to donate the books to the prison library on our arrival. Unless we are kept quite busy, I intend to use the time well and pursue my writing."

The prison librarian did accept the books, though one might wonder how many inmates checked out *Yosemite Valley Romance* or *The Road to Success, the Best Little Book in the World.*

Within a few months of his incarceration, Popham published a new book of poems in Apalachicola. *Prison Poems* sold for ten cents a copy, and contained verses such as "Love's Pen," "Dear Daddy, Please Come Home," and "First Month of Prison is a Hundred Years." He followed this with a second volume entitled *Heart Poems.*

145

Popham was released after two years, on June 30, 1928, ostensibly for his irreproachable behavior. More likely, the warden actually tried to read his smarmy poems and turned Popham loose before he could do any more damage to prison morale.

The Second Coming of William Lee Popham

Clara, Maude and William Jr. were still living in Apalachicola when Popham was released from the federal penitentiary, and Clara still held the deed to Saint George Island.

Naturally, William Lee was delighted to be released from prison, and the experience did not tarnish his reputation among friends. He was invited to dinner by his lawyer, former Senator William Hodges, on his way back to Apalachicola. In gratitude, Popham wrote a new poem in the Senator's guest book:

From Prison to Palace

Preserved within this rare abode
By happy hearts along the road
Of simple life, where knightly lords
With peasants share the rich rewards
Of honor, which a prince of men
Accords a convict from the "pen"
To sup with him and his at tea
Upon the day that he is free;
And thus, dear host, you courage bring
To one who was the "Oyster King."

On the train home, Popham opted to try for a comeback. "I finally decided that I was Divinely led to re-enter the field in which I had formerly lost, under a new corporate identify."

The *Apalachicola Times* trumpeted, "Welcome Home!," and young William Lee, Jr., recalled that nearly every man, woman and child in town came to the Apalachicola Northern train station to greet his father. The newspaper only mentioned that William Popham, Sr., had been away on an 'extended stay in Atlanta.'

The mail fraud charge still prevented him from soliciting business by means of the postal service, and also blocked him from trying to market his new books of poetry. He appealed the decision to the Post Office, and promised never to again engage in questionable business activities. In October, U.S. Postmaster General Walter Brown lifted the ban, but neither *Prison Poems* nor *Heart Poems* garnered many sales.

Despite his tribulations, William was unfazed. With a new corporation, he planned to build three thousand Oyster Huts and Seafood Restaurants that would rival the A&W hamburger franchise along new highways across the United States. The restaurants would market World-Wyde Oyster Puree, made from powdered oysters that could be shipped across the country. He conceived of Oyster Nip, a healthful beverage that would sell for five cents a glass.

The concept of marketing nutritional products nationwide was years in advance of its time, even if the newly-discovered B vitamins were being hyped

147

as 'Pep Pills.' Popham stated that he had applied for a patent for his method of powdering oysters, but there is no evidence that the U.S. Patent and Trade Office ever granted him one. Years later, in 1966, a U.S. patent was granted for powdered oysters to a team of Japanese oyster scientists.

Popham's poor land sales on Saint George Island were not due to the sentimentality of his rhymes or flawed marketing. The stock market crash of Black Tuesday, October 24,1929, impacted the entire nation. In Florida, a late hurricane compounded the damage that the Great Depression was inflicting, and a subsequent drought depleted the oyster crop.

Popham's "oyster boat" was finally sunk when he was summoned to a hearing before the U.S. Postal Department in Washington in 1936. Popham denied the new accusations of mail fraud. Short of funds, he was able to raise the required bond for Maude, but could not secure the necessary $10,000 for himself

The second trial began and ended in January, 1937. Government lawyers described a welter of confusing memoranda, contracts, charters, letters, and deeds. As before, the most serious charge was whether Popham had used the mails for fraudulent advertising. Determined not to repeat the strategic mistake of the first trial, Popham's lawyers attested to his sterling character, and then put the Oyster King on the stand to testify for himself.

Popham completely ignored the earlier, legalistic discussion. Throughout two days of direct examination and cross-examination he held the jury, lawyers, court officials, and spectators spellbound with his fervor for the oyster business. He educated the courtroom audience about the life cycle of oysters, their astonishing rate of growth, and the profit to be made with a doubling or tripling of seed oyster cultivation just as the U.S. Bureau of Fisheries stated in official publications. Popham extolled the beauty and intrinsic value of Saint George Island, the appeal of salt life, and the love for nature that no visitor could miss.

When Popham finished, his testimony had been his finest oratorical *tour de force*. Stunned, the prosecution had no rebuttal. Transfixed by the oratory, the jury quickly voted to acquit William Popham of all charges. William, Maude, and their associates were again exonerated, but left penniless, in debt to their lawyers, and still in the midst of the Great Depression. Their affairs in Apalachicola had finally, irrevocably fallen apart.

Winter sunset on a modern Saint George Island beach looking westward.

Act V. *Illigitimi non carborundum*!

Life and poems are like sand to an oyster—both are creative irritants!"

-Carol Ann Duffy

At the conclusion of the second trial, William Lee and Maude Popham were free but penniless, living on $15 a week that his brother Arthur was able to send. William could not pay his legal bills, and ceded Saint George Island to his defense attorneys in lieu of monetary payment.

The defense team had been run by former State Senator William Hodges (he was not related to the Florida Shell Fish Commissioner), and the Senator was not interested in holding island property. On his team was a young lawyer named Clyde Atkinson, who received part of the title, but realized that there would be no development for years. Senator Hodges' wife, Margaret, had heard her brother William ("Bill") Wilson speak fondly of Saint George Island. The Senator sold his interest to Wilson. Years later, Wilson and Atkinson would help realize William Popham's dream of developing the island.

Clara Popham died shortly after the trial ended. With the Depression continuing, there was no hope of making a comeback in Apalachicola. The oyster empire William Lee had built was gone, and the packing houses were in other people's hands. The Pophams had sold all the properties they owned during the trial.

150

Having sold the Chapman House and their farm in Tampa, the family took to the road in 1938 seeking new opportunities. They first followed other itinerant Southerners to Detroit. Finding no prospects there, William got the idea that mining in Nevada was going to boom. He conceived the idea of parlaying interests in hard, abrasive mineral called carborundum into a new fortune. With World War II starting, there would be need for industrial abrasives. However, the natural mineral was only associated with meteorite craters, and essentially any amount needed could be made in chemical plants.

When his dream of becoming wealthy with carborundum failed, the Pophams moved on to Los Angeles. William became a realtor and lived out his life in California, never again finding the prominence he had known as evangelist, promoter, and mayor of Apalachicola. With the advent of radio, popularity of the Chautauqua circuit also diminished. Popham's heyday had passed. He supported the family through real estate ventures, but died of uremia in 1953. Maude survived him, living until 1980. William, Jr., changed his name to Parker, primarily because friends in California found 'Popham' quaint and hard to pronounce.

William Lee Popham never forgot his romance with Saint George Island and the oyster industry. He firmly believed that hard work would be rewarded with success, and that he would make a comeback. His mastery of the spoken word and gift for poetry would be the ticket, if only he kept his faith, his deep belief in the power of divine love, and his abiding respect for women and home. His beliefs were rooted in his Kentucky boyhood, his

151

family ties, his church, and a zealous optimism that expressed itself in every business venture. We do not need to ask what he believed, for he wrote his every thought in poems, lectures and sermons.

In *A Poet's Walk* from 1910, William Lee Popham talked about wandering on a mountain, hoping to view the sunset, but losing his way as night fell. Though he became fearful, birds began to sing, and he heard voices of hope and happiness calling to him:

> Be not frightened of the dark;
> The Savior guides you still.
> Darkness now precedes the dawn
> For 'tis God's holy will.
> Tho' earth is dressed in shadows,
> The sky's a starry awning;
> There never was a night so dark
> It did not have a dawning.
> One, the bird of happiness,
> And one the bird of hope
> Doth promise thee that soon the moon
> Will light the mountain slope.

Hope and faith always sustained William Lee Popham, and there is no evidence that he ever despaired, whether facing ruin of his enterprises, trials for mail fraud, or the blocking of his ability to use the postal service for his advertising. Undaunted and a born entrepreneur, William Lee Popham saw no reason to change. He was always about to succeed with his next grand scheme.

In his own words, "Were it not for hope, I would have surrendered to failure a thousand times."

To some people, William Lee Popham was a fraud and scoundrel. To others, he was a respected and engaging member of his church and community. Years later, a business associate declared, "Popham was crucified." Another long-time resident of Apalachicola exclaimed, "If they had only left poor Mr. Popham alone he would have made something out of the island and out of this town. You just can't help wondering where we would be by now."

It would take another thirty years to truly begin developing Saint George Island in the way William Lee Popham had envisioned in 1916, as a place where ordinary people could relax in the surf, watch pelicans and dolphins chasing mullet along the shore, refresh their souls while basking in the Florida sun, and contemplate dining on steamed, baked, broiled or raw oysters with a flirt of hot red pepper sauce.

Epilogue

"I've learned that there's three things in this world a man can't predict: women, hurricanes, and the mind of a shrimp!"

-A Franklin County Fisherman

William Lee Popham left a legacy not only in Apalachicola but in the country. The federal trial of Popham vs. The United States became a landmark precedent for mail fraud. The entire thousand-page transcript can be found in libraries in the U.S. Fifth Circuit Court of Appeals. Nearly every book Popham and Maude wrote is available in the U.S. Library of Congress.

As the Popham family drove away from Apalachicola and Saint George Island, economic conditions were bleak. The Great Depression continued, and the United States began preparing for a second great war that seemed inevitable in 1939. Nobody was interested in real estate, particularly on a barrier island with no city water or electricity, no bridge across four miles of bay, and 80 miles from the nearest population center. Bill Wilson held the title to Saint George Island and regarded it the same way George Saxon had, a cash drain that he needed to sell. But nobody was buying in those bleak years.

Presaging the age of interstate travel by automobile, the John Gorrie Bridge between Apalachicola and Eastpoint was completed in 1935. It was to be an essential link in a new highway called U.S. 98 that would link towns along the Gulf.

154

U.S. 98 connected to U.S. Highway 319, so that citizens of Tallahassee could finally drive to the Gulf bay shores in an hour or two.

Despite the new roads along the coast, little development took place on Saint George Island before World War II. Abruptly, the US government leased Saint George Island from Mr. Wilson, employing it as landing practice for the D-Day invasion of Normandy for troops in the nearby Camp Gordon Johnson, as well as for aerial strafing practice. After the war was over, Wilson received title back from the government, but conveyed half to Clyde Atkinson again. No matter who owned the island, it seemed that having an attorney as a partner was a good, defensive idea!

In 1951, Wilson and Atkinson formed a company called Saint George Island Gulf Beaches. Only then was the island platted with housing development in mind. Partly because of opposition from ecologically-minded interests, who understood that over-development could destroy the shellfish industry, the plats were kept large and most of the development was limited to single family cottages. High-rise condominiums can never be built on Saint George Island.

The Franklin County Board of Commissioners was aware that access to Saint George Island would increase property tax revenue for the county, and revenue was badly needed. Colonel Bryant Patton, owner of the Apalachicola Fish and Oyster Company, was elected to the Florida House of Representatives starting in 1949. He helped secure authorization that included shipping channels from Apalachicola and Eastpoint and ferry service to the

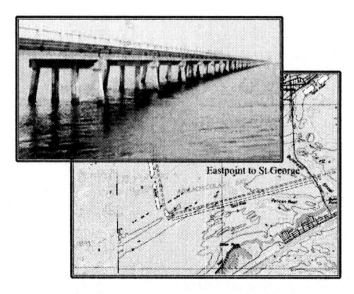

Eastpoint to St George

**State Representative Bryant Patton helped
pass legislation to permit Florida counties to
fund bridge construction. The first bridge was
finished in 1965. After the new bridge was
completed in 2008, the old one was converted to
a fishing pier.**

Gulf Beaches. Crucially, the legislation allowed
counties to finance bridges to islands.

Daily ferry service for cars and passengers to
Saint George Island did not begin until 1955.
Residents of Apalachicola also got approval for
harbor improvement, part of which was the
federally-funded dredging of a permanent pass
through the island, which was completed in 1957
and named Bob Sikes Cut. "The Cut" allows
shrimpers and fishermen quick access to the Gulf.
However, it also allows high salinity Gulf water to
enter the bay, which could potentially harm the
oysters in years of drought when the river fails to

deliver adequate fresh water to the estuary. However, salt water incursion is offset by the tidal currents that move from the east to the west, making The Cut more of an exit than an entrance.

Engineering surveys for a bridge were begun in 1955, and $4 million in funding for the first bridge to Saint George Island was secured in 1962 as a joint project between Franklin County and the state Development Commission. Originally, a $2 toll was required for auto traffic.

To compound the problem with water flow in the Apalachicola estuary, a dam was proposed in 1947, and in 1957 the Jim Woodruff dam was opened a hundred miles upstream near the Georgia border. There has been a perpetual battle to maintain adequate fresh water flow to the bay from Georgia and Alabama ever since.

Despite the ferry service to Saint George Island, few homes were built in the '50's. In addition to limited access, there was no electricity or water supply other than from rainwater or hand-pumped wells on the island. That changed when the Bryant Patton toll bridge was completed in 1965. A power line was strung on poles across the bay, and lot sales on Saint George Island increased rapidly, as did prices of the lots. Within a decade, island property taxes became a major source of funding for Franklin County roads and schools. It had taken 50 years to put in place all the elements needed to realize William Popham's dream of sharing Saint George Island with the citizens of Florida.

A parcel of land that became part of the Julian Bruce State Park was donated to the state in 1963.

Bill Wilson's death in 1969 left Clyde Atkinson most influential in further development. He sold most of the East and West ends of the island to John Stocks in 1971, who founded Leisure Properties to develop that part of the island. To raise money, Stocks and his partners sold a large parcel of land to the State, which completed the 2,000 acres needed for Dr. Julian Bruce State Park on the East end of Saint George Island.

John Stocks and partners including Tallahassee attorney Gene Brown gradually developed The Plantation, the private community between 12th Street West and Bob Sikes Cut. Clyde Atkinson sold properties in Saint George Island Gulf Beaches to other realtors, who developed the middle part of the island. Sales increased rapidly in the 1970's and 80's, and the island began to take on its modern ambience of beachside homes interspersed with sea oats, oak laurel and contorted yellow pines.

Permanent residents of Saint George Island, Eastpoint, and Apalachicola have always lived with vagaries imposed by storms, droughts and financial crises. In 2005, the storm surge brought on by Hurricane Dennis silted over the oyster bottoms and damaged waterfront on both sides of the bay just when real estate prices seemed to have no limits. Before the bay could recover from the storm, a financial crisis knocked home prices to one-third of their former, inflated value. Speculators had no way to recover expenses and many followed William Popham into financial ruin. The storm coincided with a period of drought that is still decimating the oyster industry.

Fraud or Futurist: You Be the Jury

It seems odd that the federal government would have brought charges against William Popham in the remote town of Apalachicola, considering events going on in the rest of Florida. The land boom around Miami began with the completion of the Florida East Coast Railway, offering escape from New York in 1913. Finished in 1915, the Dixie Highway allowed motorists to leave the cold winters of Chicago and upper Michigan.

These routes from the north by rail and automobile led to a massive wave of real estate speculation that collapsed in 1925 when a ship sank and blocked flow of construction materials into Miami harbor. Then the hurricane of 1926 made northern investors skittish about prospects for land sales in Miami. Businessmen lost fortunes worth hundreds of millions as the building and real estate industries imploded in a downfall that foreshadowed the 1929 crash on Wall Street and Great Depression.

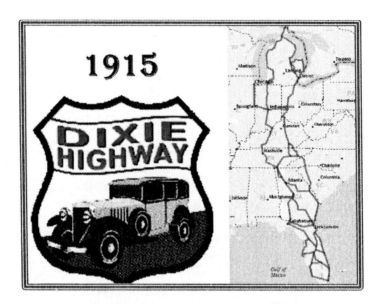

The Dixie Highway, promoted by Florida developer and visionary headlight manufacturer Carl Fisher, was a system of North-South roadways. Built between 1915 and 1927, it connected roads from Michigan to Miami and complemented East Coast road and rail systems that extended to Key West.

Given that greater context, here are the specific charges the US government brought against 'The Oyster King':

"The defendant, William Lee Popham, having devised a scheme for obtaining money by means of false and fraudulent representations, for the purpose of executing such scheme placed a letter therein sufficiently described in a post office, to be sent and delivered by the post office establishment of the United States.

The representations charged to be false consisted of statements to the effect that said defendant owned lands, especially submerged lands, which were suitable for the propagation and cultivation of oysters, near Apalachicola, Fla., from which purchasers would realize exceedingly large returns upon their investments.

The elements of an offense under the postal code are (a) a scheme devised or intended to be devised to defraud, or for obtaining money or property by means of false pretenses; and (b) for the purpose of executing such scheme, or attempting to do so, the placing of any letter in any post office of the United States to be sent or delivered by the post office establishment."

William Popham's first love was not the oyster industry; it was a romance with developing Saint George Island as a 'City by the Sea.' Oysters did provide a possible income to shareholders, but that was secondary to land sales. Consider a specific statement in one of Popham's real estate brochures:

"Most of the few Florida islands are today priceless and not for sale...the beach is good; an island beach is better, a sea-island beach is best...For a limited time, you can get your 'choice lot' for $150...it is not unreasonable to expect these very lots to sell, perhaps in the not distant future, for one thousand dollars each ..."

A poem illustrated his romantic concept:

When Eve walked in the Garden
And Adam by her side
He the happy groom

And she the lovely bride
Bothered not with bathing suits
Nor styles of oddly notion
They daily took a plunge
In the grand old ocean.
And methinks that garden
Of God's approving smile
Was on the lovely shores
Of St. George's Isle.

So of course there was mail fraud, as no one else has ever suggested that the Garden of Eden was on Saint George Island!

The island William Popham bought for $35,000 in 1920 was appraised at $650,000 in 1926 and sold that year for $300,000. The forced sale was due to the intervention of the federal government in a suit that was not brought by Popham's share-holders. Today is the distant future, and there has been a bridge since 1965. Present values of lots on Saint George Island begin at $50,000 for the least desirable, interior places, and can exceed $1 million for premier lots on the Gulf beaches.

How true was the U.S. government's principle charge that Popham fraudulently represented the amount of income that could be obtained from oyster harvesting? In his earliest mailing, Popham cited a report from the U.S. Bureau of Fisheries that stated that every barrel of oyster shell planted in a suitable bay would return two to three barrels of oysters after two years. He announced plans to plant 200,000 barrels of shell in order to return 600,000 barrels of harvest. At three gallons per barrel and $2 per gallon, he calculated that oyster cultivation could produce an income of up to $200 a month.

There is no doubt that these claims were exaggerated, but it is also true that Popham was taking the most optimistic view, as he always did in every endeavor. In contrast, Shell Fish Commissioner Hodges took the most pessimistic view, noting that the state of Florida did not produce that many oysters.

Hodges failed to point out two key facts. Firstly, Apalachicola Bay is the best oyster habitat in the state, and usually produces more than 80% of all oysters from Florida. At peak production, the bay yields 90% of all oysters harvested in the state. Secondly, when Popham made his claim, few oystermen were planting shells, much less cultivating oysters on sunken platforms. Most relied on natural shell beds and the shucked shells were sold to be used to construct highway and railroad beds. In contrast, Popham not only planted hundreds of thousands of barrels of oyster shell that he obtained from the Acme Oyster Packing Company, he also hired crews to cultivate oysters on bundles of oak trees set up on prime oyster bottoms around Saint George Island. He truly was farming under water, unlike others who were hunting on the natural beds.

The oyster harvest from Apalachicola Bay in the early 1920's yielded revenue of about $160,000 per year to the oystermen, but higher prices were obtained by oyster packers who sold on the retail market, as Popham did. The market value did not exceed $1 million until 1962, and in peak years can now produce $5 million.

So, were the figures Popham used fraudulent? It is true that he overestimated income based on what working oystermen could obtain from natural oyster bars when they did not reseed much shell. But that is not what Popham was doing. His crews not only deposited spent shell on the natural reefs, they constructed thousands of acres of new bars in suitable habitat. Whereas only about 7,000 acres of the bay harbored natural oyster beds, the US Bureau of Fisheries estimated that up to 40% of the bay could be productive. That would be a massive increase in acreage, even today.

The only man in the courtroom during the first trial who knew these facts was William Popham, and, on advice of his lawyers, he did not testify. The futurist remained mum, and let his lawyers argue legal points on his behalf. The jury heard from the State Shell Fish Commissioner, who merely noted that Popham was promising more oysters than the state was producing. To them, the case for fraud seemed, like an oyster on the incoming tide, 'open and shut.'

What do you think?

As William Popham sat in the US Federal Penitentiary in Atlanta, writing two more books of poems, the economy of Florida-and the demand for oysters- was collapsing. He did not win release until 1929, when the entire country was falling into its worst economic depression. It seems likely that Popham's dream to develop Saint George Island was premature. It would happen eventually, but it needed a 'Bridge to Somewhere' and a coastal highway system. There were to be chains of fast-food restaurants along those highways as Popham envisioned, but none of them featured oysters on the bill of fare.

Popham indeed 'Saw through a glass darkly,' as he frequently said, but he did see through the glass when others could not. He lost a fortune that may have been close to two million dollars, but then, the developers of Coral Gables and Miami Beach lost hundreds of millions, and most were never accused of fraud.

Through it all, the oystermen of Apalachicola and Eastpoint just kept on tonging, never getting much ahead but always having the great bay to feed their families. None of them ever called Mr. Popham 'The Oyster King.' They knew better.

A sunset view over modern Saint George Island taken from a kayak on the Gulf of Mexico.

Information Sources

Anonymous. United States Circuit Court of Appeals Fifth Circuit, No. 4698: William Lee Popham, Plaintiff-in-error, Vs. United States of America, Defendant-in-error. Transcript of Record. T.J. Appleyard, Publisher, 1925, 1167 pp.

Estes, Maude Miller. *Love Poems and the Boyhood of Kentucky's Poet, Being the Life-Story of William Lee Popham.* World Supply Company (Mayes Printers). Louisville, KY, 1910, 92 pp.

Huxley, Thomas Henry. *Oysters and the Oyster Question.* English Illustrated Magazine, 1893-94, pp. 47-55 and 112-121.

Lockwood, Samuel. *The Natural History of the Oyster I and II.* Popular Science Monthly 1874, vol. 6, pp. 1-20 and 157-173.

Monod, Olivier, *Real Estate Sales Trends - St. George Island & Cape San Blas - 1920 to 1985: Making History Twice.* Anchor Realty blog. Internet URL, http://www.florida-beach.com Verified February 2, 2013.

Moore, Henry Frank. *Oysters and Oyster-Culture with Notes on Clam Culture.* Publication 349, U.S. Commission of Fish and Fisheries, 1897.

Popham, William Lee. *Silver Gems in Seas of Gold.* Broadway Publishing Co., Broadway, NY, 1910, 222 pp.

Proctor, Samuel. *William Jennings Bryan and the University of Florida.* Florida Historical Quarterly 1960, vol. 39, 1-15.

Rogers, William Warren. *Outposts on the Gulf. Saint George Island and Apalachicola from Early exploration to World War II*. University of West Florida Press, Pensacola, FL, 1986, 297 pp.

Rogers, William Warren. *The Power of the Written Word and the Spoken Word in the Rise and Fall of William Lee Popham*. The Florida Historical Quarterly, Vol. 76, No. 3 (Winter, 1998), pp. 265-296.

Rogers, William Warren and Willis, Lee, III. *At The Water's Edge. A Pictorial and Narrative History of Apalachicola and Franklin County*. The Donning Company Publishers, Virginia Beach, VA, 1997, 176 pp.

The United States Library of Congress, catalog records for William Lee Popham and Maude Miller Estes.

Image Sources

Historical images of Apalachicola area are from the archives of the Florida Department of State, Division of Library and Information Sciences, at the Florida Memory URL: www.floridamemory.com

Photographs by Lewis Hine are from the US National Archives, http://arcweb.archives.gov

Other images were created by the author from non-copyrighted sources. Sketches of sea turtles and bejeweled fish were done by Katy Hargrove in 1995.